PLANT MEDICINE
MYSTERY SCHOOL

PLANT MEDICINE
MYSTERY SCHOOL

Volume I: The Superhero Healing Powers of
Psychotropic Plants

Tina Kat Courtney

MetanoiaPress

Plant Medicine Mystery School Volume I: The Superhero Healing Powers of Psychotropic Plants. Copyright © 2021 Tina Kat Courtney. All Rights Reserved.

Published by Metanoia Press, www.metanoia.press
Cover & Interior Art by August Hall, www.augusthallprints.com
Book Design & Editing by Suzanne Winters

Printed in the United States of America
First Printing: October 2021
ISBN: 978-1-7336011-5-3

Table of Contents

Dedications

I BOW IN HUMBLE RECOGNITION and reverence to all the teachers and shamans who came before me, guarding and carrying these medicines throughout time. Most especially, thank you to my first teacher and second father, Howard Lawler, for seeing what I couldn't see inside myself, and for showing me the path to Heaven was always within.

This book is dedicated to the plants who saved my life, and to whom I would gladly dedicate mine in gratitude:

Ayahuasca
Chacruna
Huachuma

And all the Master Plants who continuously heal, uplift, humble, and mesmerize me.

This book would not exist without the talents and support of the Metanoia crew, most notably the amazing Mobius, Suzanne, and August.

I also give tackle hugs to my powerhouse partner Laura, forehead bumps to my soul kitty Prana, and endless love and gratitude to Abby, the best medicine partner in the multiverse. And to the ever-expanding and oh-so-precious plant medicine tribe that has trusted us to create love and safety in this space: Endless gratitude for the love, support, and inspiration you give us every day. Let's keep raising the vibration of duality into nonduality and bring heart-spaced healing to everyone we encounter.

Prologue / Author's Intro

FIFTEEN YEARS AGO, when I had my first cup of Ayahuasca, I never in a million centuries guessed that in less than two decades, everyone and their grandmothers would be called to work with psychotropic plant medicines. When I returned from the Amazon from my first cycle of ceremonies, all bright-eyed and lit-up over the magic of these medicines, I was the wacky LA girl who had taken some drugs in the jungle and thought she found the secrets of the universe. No one had heard of this mysterious brew, and almost no one in my vast professional and personal circles had any interest, despite my urging otherwise. I felt destined to have discovered a best kept secret, one that undoubtedly saved my life, and felt pretty damn certain I was the hippie outcast that would die singing the praises of this wild and transformative jungle brew.

There was a single moment, however, where I realized things were changing. About six years into my obsession, I sat next to my mother at a blackjack table in the small Nevada border town where she had resided since I had left home for college. By then, I was the Ayahuasca poster child; I had drank hundreds of times and had manifested multiple teachers and adventures, still clinging to the identity of an outsider who had found her life's mission. Three overgrown frat guys plopped down next to us, clutching their American beers and cigarettes, and both my mother and I quietly judged them.

My angel mama–ever the champion of her only daughter–had, since day one of my Amazonian discovery, done her best to support the hairbrained path I gave my heart and soul to. She didn't understand the all-in mission; although she was a child of the 60s, she chose Elvis over the Beatles and didn't even enjoy the buzz of a glass of wine, let alone a multidimensional psychedelic blowout. So she humored my nonstop ceremony stories, but didn't suppose this shamanism thing was ever going to really pay the bills.

In a way, our frat friends sitting at our table that evening would change everything.

We played a few hands of blackjack, and I secretly prayed none of them would flirt with me. I loathed the attention of unconscious, immature men who assumed my friendly nature meant I desired their questions and banter. I had already written a story in my overactive mind around who they were. I kept my eyes on my cards and cracked a joke or two quietly to my mother.

One of the gentlemen, completely out of the blue, caught my attention by asking me, "Have you ever done Ayahuasca?"

My dumbfounded stare caused him to quickly qualify his question. "I'm so sorry, I don't know why I asked that."

This wasn't the first time a random new acquaintance would ask me that million dollar question; I often felt like I wore a visible button that said, "Ask me about Ayahuasca!" But this was "next level." I felt instantly schooled about my horrible judgments, completely awed by how the medicine used me to help sincere seekers find their way, and this time, fully aware of my mother's shock and awe.

Turns out, this lovely being was from Utah. He had sat in an underground ceremony the previous year with a shaman from Peru, and deeply desired more experiences with Ayahuasca. Something within pushed him to ask this total stranger if she could help.

I did help, of course, by giving this kind soul the name and location of my trusted Amazonian home; he did indeed take my advice, and had his own life-changing journey. But that was the moment that made me realize that Ayahuasca was going mainstream.

So here we are, on the precipice of the total psychedelic renaissance, with corp-ra-delic companies springing up as fast as a psychedelic blastoff, living in a world where you are now in the minority if you haven't heard of and at least considered trying one of these magical plant medicines. The issue is no longer awareness, but sacredness, as the Western world is in full swing doing what it does best: Profiting off of the world's need to heal and awaken, and laying claim to the magic that has always existed in nature.

I have watched with genuine joy and fear as Ayahuasca and her plant partners have popped up—well, everywhere—sometimes spoken about with integrity and reverence, but normally full of myths, fear-mongering, and marketing mumbo jumbo. I was recently interviewed about the PTSD capabilities of Aya on Fox News Radio, of all places. That means she's officially everywhere.

There's an ever-expanding repertoire of books, podcasts, blogs, and videos about working with Aya, and most of them encapsulate one of two perspectives: Folks sharing about their personal experiences, and scientists and corporations sharing the chemical structure and efficacies. In most cases, the plants are spoken about as objects, as substances, very akin to supplements or pharmaceutical drugs. Everyone has a desired outcome, a core reason for wanting to either work with or capitalize on these medicines, yet very few acknowledge one extraordinarily important factor.

Ayahuasca, Mushrooms, Iboga, Huachuma, Ganja, and the entire plant kingdom... these are conscious, aware, and sentient beings. This is precisely why they captivate us with their power and intelligence. They are not to be used for any level of personal gain; they are to be partnered with, to be respected and revered, and to be approached via a mutual relationship. This is why they have often been vilified; they are far too wise and dynamic to ever follow the scientific method of repeated and expected results. Our past history has shown that when something is unpredictable and unable to be controlled by "superior" humans, it/they can quickly be labeled as dangerous and be ostracized by the powers that be, who then choose to take away our human right to connect with nature and discover who we really are.

This right here is the reason this book exists. I am unspeakably blessed to have been chosen as a partner to these powerhouse beings, but because they do not have voices themselves, they have tapped various messengers to please remind the world that we are dealing with living, conscious beings, and that if we do not show respect and spaciousness to them, our healing, and possibly even our very existence, will be at risk.

All hail the psychedelic renaissance. It's an unbelievably good problem to have that these medicines are so prevalent, so in-demand, that some of us feel compelled to speak out about safety and reverence. I am honored to offer the perspective of who and what these medicines are from someone who has forged all-in relationships with them, approaching each one with this intention: Show me who you are. And in return, through my personal filter, I will share that with whomever wants to know you, too.

This is a book about the superheroes of the plant world; the entheogens that, by my estimation, are indeed here to save the planet. At their core, they all bring us back to a remembrance of our divinity and omnipotence, and our connection to this incredible yet deeply ailing orb. It's pretty obvious to many of us that if we don't get in right relations with our beloved, conscious, Mother Earth, she will cease to tolerate our existence much longer, as we are jeopardizing her health and safety more every day.

My hope is that these words help you forge a more conscious and respectful bond with these absolutely magical plant beings. My hope is that you discover more about how they deeply wish to help us heal and awaken, and the safe and reverent ways to do that. And my hope is that this book helps in some way to bring us all back into a mutual, loving relationship with the planet and her children.

Let us claim our right to be whole, conscious, and free. And let us do so by bowing in humble awe to the loving power of the Earth and her plant medicine powerhouses.

Thank you for reading and for being a part of the Plant Medicine Tribe.

Testimony #1: Elana Horwich

Author of *Meal and a Spiel, How to be a Badass in the Kitchen*
Chef, Writer, Plant Medicine Lover

I first embarked on a journey with Ayahuasca to finally face a lifelong depression that plagued me and my entire family for generations. After having tried so many other modalities including antidepressants, Ayahuasca was a last ditch effort. An act of desperation. I was terrified to work with her because I had little experience with psychedelics and was very scared of both throwing up and passing out. My body was very sensitive, and I wasn't sure it could withstand such strong medicine. In fact, I had suffered profound chronic fatigue, light-headed weakness, and occasional fainting for decades, despite adopting every holistic and nutritional possibility. I was accustomed to tough love from an early age and expected her to deliver what I knew. What I have received from Ayahuasca, from that first time until now (at least a dozen sittings later), is pure nurturing love. She always takes me to my edge, but never abandons me in the process. She acknowledges my fear and helps me work with it by holding my hand every step of the way. This is not what many people experience with Ayahuasca, yet she is also known for giving you what you need. By showing up as a gentle nurturing motherly figure, she showed me how to nurture myself. In the process, I have gained enormous compassion for the parts of me that needed healing.

Almost immediately Ayahuasca let me know that I had trauma in my nervous system and this was why my body had become overly sensitive to various stimuli. Our first sessions were all about rewiring my nervous system, and my brain. She pointed to an early childhood accident that had left me with PTSD. I learned that much of the trauma I was carrying in this body was in fact linked to the enormous fear my Jewish ancestors had passed down from narrowly escaping murder throughout the ages and from those perished in the Holocaust. As we worked to relieve the remnants of a traumatic ancestral legacy, my body strengthened. She gently let me know that the reason that my body and emotions were suffering so was because I had a broken heart, cracked in childhood and then cracked again and again as a teenager and adult. As she showed me the way to heal my heart, I felt a fierceness in my physical and emotional body that I hadn't experienced in decades. *She showed me how to be strong in the surrender so my heart could heal into wise softness.*

One of the greatest gifts given to me by Ayahuasca was her gentle insistence I use other plant medicines to help with the healing she had in store for me. She pointed me to San Pedro so I could receive the loving touch of the divine masculine. To Kambo to build fire in my body, strengthen every system in it and turn me into a true warrior. To Peyote for deeper understanding and removal of ancestral trauma and personal violations embedded in my belly, aka my emotional brain. To Bobinsana to help me feel all the sadness I was carrying in my heart and transform it into a loving story. To Sage for showing me how to protect my energy by paying attention to and honoring my feelings. To Hapé to help me ground, center myself, and build my immune system. To Mambe to help my body digest high-frequency nourishment in a low-impact way. She brought me back to Mushrooms to help me further physically remove ancestral fear out of my nervous system and open my heart even more to the love around me. I have learned that the medicine and consciousness of plants is not second to humans, but rather they are the greatest teachers and doctors we have available to us.

Elana Horwich
www.elanahorwich.com

Mystery #1: Everybody Wants to Be a Shaman, Except Those That Are

The Birth of an Unlikely Medicine Mama

Every mystery school is founded on the person or people who are ready and willing to pass down the secrets of the universe. There is no basis of credibility in the universally sacred container without the knowledge that the messenger knows of what they speak. So allow me to briefly be a tad indulgent and share a sliver or two of my plant-centric journey.

I'm going to share some extremely intimate details of my life that not even my closest friends and family are completely aware of. I'm doing this to give a personal context to the magic of sacred plants, to their potency, and to the wild and wonderful journey I've walked in order to know the things I will share throughout this book.

Mostly, however, I'm going to honor my commitment of integrity and transparency I've forged with my plant partners. They have taught me that truth is the only way out of the chaos. So I first have to show up real, vulnerable, and all-in. Before I take you on the journey of understanding the plants, I'll first have the courage to write bloody.

Out of the 7.8 billion people on the planet, I am easily one of the least likely humans to be birthing this book. There is nothing extraordinary about my talents or intellect. I wasn't born into a shamanic family or culture, and there was no obvious indication that I would someday be authorized by the spirit world to be a sacred messenger and a plant whisperer. Although I grew up in the majestic mountains of Montana, I had zero connection to plant consciousness. In fact, I counted the hours before I was to escape from that isolating, boring-and-bonkers small town I grew up in. I couldn't keep a houseplant alive. I envisioned being a therapist or a veterinarian. Most of all, I just wanted to get the hell out of Hicksville.

Here's the painful truth about my early years: The topic I thought about most was death. I had the outward exterior of a normal, cheerful, friendly girl-next-door type, and by my 20s I had an amazing career as a video game producer for Disney. I had moved through health issues from my childhood (an underdeveloped respiratory system that was uber-prone to pneumonia, asthma, and related illnesses) and appeared strong and resilient. But my smile was the type that masked a seething black hole of suffering, alienation, rage, and debilitating sadness. I took immense comfort in knowing that death would bring relief, so I fantasized a lot about finally escaping this earthly hell.

There was absolutely no tangible, tell-tale reason for this darkness inside me. I had no significant stories of abuse that made me feel justified for this insatiable urge to escape, so I tended to exaggerate or outright fabricate past events to try to make sense of my emotions. This made the depression far worse, as I also ended up feeling like a total and utter fraud. Yes, bad things had happened to me. But most of my tribe had survived far worse events and legitimately did not appear damaged beyond all repair. There had to be something horrifically wrong with me.

A bipolar diagnosis in my twenties actually gave me joy. I finally had something I could point to that proved I was indeed broken. Only I didn't really tell anyone. I would rather tell the made-up stories of suffering than own the vulnerability of what was actually going on.

Only the men I allowed into my intimate sphere had the true opportunity of seeing the honest space of breakdown I had attained. I exuded a strong, together exterior, and yet behind closed doors I was the proverbial hot mess.

It was therefore a very natural, unconscious decision to repeatedly turn to alcohol and recreational drugs for escape. I started with LSD at age 19. I adored the incredible mental freedom and empowerment it gave me. I felt the doors in my mind burst open and all this potential and joy and playfulness and hope came rising up inside me. But then the moment sobriety came sludging back in, my heart would close, my mind would grow dark, and reality became the unwanted visitor that would never really leave.

A frightful trip on LSD that forced me to expose my lack of integrity and love for myself put the kibosh on future journeys: When I was 20, I had a boyfriend that loved to journey with me, and we would do so at the USC campus, trudging through the brick-covered buildings and talking to the light posts and statues. One night, we tripped at the top of a parking structure, and I went into my first ever dark night of the soul on psychedelics. Fear took over. I went into a psychotic state where all I could do was repeat "You're in love with a movie," over and over. It was my way of calling out my lack of authenticity. To my utter shock and awe, he told me, "I know, and I love you anyway." That made the experience even more unbearable, because I couldn't fathom how someone could know I lacked integrity and still love me. So I promptly got rid of the boyfriend and no longer embraced altered spaces. That perspective would last several years.

Eventually, I found MDMA (Molly, ecstasy). That absolutely changed my life. I was able to view the world around me without judgment; I started to find a spark of self-love and curiosity for the darkness. But over-usage and a total lack of reverence for set and setting—care and context—turned my savior into a nightmare, too. I became more anxious, more agitated, and more afraid of the world with the one substance that was supposed to give me relief.

The only thing that gave me any semblance of comfort was alcohol; that potent, dulling, numbing addiction our culture is so wildly fond of. It took me years to go there, but when I did, I went full throttle. Planning my day around the alcohol I would consume was normal. I cared more about the wine in the rack than the food in the cupboards.

This is how I spent my twenties. I was a high functioning, seemingly a-okay woman with a great job, a slew of beautiful relationships, an amazing tribe of friends, a loving family, and a secret habit of drugs, alcohol, and an eating disorder: bulimia. Oh, did I forget to mention the eating disorder? Yet another shameful, hidden element of my day-to-day.

Inside, I had an unshakable, polarizing case of self-loathing; even though my beautiful parents filled me up with confidence and love and told me I could do anything. Even though I had a relatively normal upbringing. Even though on paper, it seemed like I should be overjoyed, living the dream, and fully embracing life.

Instead, I constantly managed anxiety and fear. I sought to control the chaos and pain around me via bulimia (which also expressed my utterly insane level of hatred for my miraculous, incredible body). I had edgy highs of mania that frightened me with their sheer power, and shockingly dark lows that consumed me with thoughts of suicide. But you likely wouldn't know that if we were friends back then. You would have only known the convincing fake smile I offered one and all. At least I think it was convincing. Maybe I was fooling no one. I wasn't fooling myself.

Another Life Saved in the Jungle

As my thirtieth year ushered in, I fell in love with a devious bad boy who was a bigwig in the film industry. I'll call him Rocket. He created special FX for horror films, and he was the perfect narcissistic dreamboat to distract me from my own issues and encouraged me to make my whole life about him. This was a pattern. I was all-in yet again.

Little did I know he was a sheep in wolf's clothing. Although famous for womanizing, creating realistic death scenes and horror movie demons, and for rarely being sober, he would also be the man who brought me home to Ayahuasca. He was edgy AF, but he led me to salvation.

21

One afternoon, we sat across from each other noshing nondescript salads, and he said the word, "Ayahuasca." I did not know this word, but everything in me responded.

Rocket and I, we were no stranger to altered spaces, although these were more of the benign Molly variety along with heavy doses of alcohol. At this stage of my life, I was so racked with fear that I normally faked being in altered spaces from taking cocaine and MDMA in order to avoid the discomfort of the breakdown that was becoming inevitable with me; everyone around me would pop the pills and snort the lines, and I'd appear to do the same but instead pocket or brush off the substance. None were the wiser. My erratic behavior already reeked of anything but sobriety, and I had had enough frightening nose-dives with drugs, I couldn't risk more breakdowns. So this was one more thing I could hate about myself; the fraud lived on.

But this Ayahuasca thing—Rocket had my attention. He was headed to the jungle in a few weeks. And I knew immediately I was going with him. Twenty-one days later we were in his limo to the airport. I had adventure on my mind; I also had zero idea what I was about to experience.

When I arrived at the rustic, somewhat horrifying Amazonian lodge, I became completely confronted with my self-hatred. It arose in me like an uncaged, rabid puma, and every corner of false joy I tried to hide in was immediately exposed.

The night before the first ceremony, I announced to the assembled crew that I hated myself, that I couldn't handle this intensity, and that I wanted to leave. I confessed I had no idea the process would start before I drank a drop of Ayahuasca. This terrified me. It was obvious this was not "fun times on drugs." I doubted my feeble sense of sanity would be able to survive this trip. Rocket, too, was obsessed with my fragility, and excessively touted that I would not be able to handle what was coming, and he deeply regretted dragging me along. Once again, I did a bang-up job at choosing a partner with compassion and kindness.

One of the shamans there—a man who would later become a teacher and a father figure—said to me simply,

"Sweetheart, trust me, you are perfect for this work."

And boy howdy did it feel like work. I could already feel this was shadow work. Soul work. I had not signed up for a recreational romp.

So I trusted him. I stayed. And what happened in three ceremonies down there in that remote part of the Amazon, a world away from my surface-skimming, turbocharged Los Angeles life, would completely and utterly transform the rest of my existence.

Ayahuasca gave me what I had never thought possible: She made me feel, down to my very core, that I could indeed be happy. That I could heal, I could make peace with my suffering, and I could be genuine, honest, stable, and free.

It was going to take more than three ceremonies to get there, but I didn't care if it took a million. I knew it was possible. I knew she was the one to help me. And the fire that lit inside of me that Earth day in April 2006 has never—not once—disappeared.

The journey from then on? It's been one hell of a wild ride. I have spent months and months in the jungle studying with various teachers. I then partnered with a respected shaman in the United States and began my first apprenticeship, which I ended abruptly two and a half years later because it just wasn't the old school, traditional lineage training I was looking for.

Shortly thereafter, I met the man who would become my teacher. It took the medicine several months of coaxing him out of an assumption that I was a bimbo who couldn't hack it; he finally approached me and offered an apprenticeship. I said yes, then no, then HELL YES.

It's a long-ass crazy story that maybe someday I will put down on paper, but suffice to say I never gave up. I have, however, given up relationships, a career as a video game producer, a marketing company I co-founded, sacred friendships, and a genuine sense of safety to do this work. I've faced the most terrorizing aspects of my psyche, and continue to do so. I've experienced death and rebirth numerous times. And I've continued this incredible love affair with multiple plants that I now know better than any human being in my life. They are my friends, lovers, allies, and butt-kicking feet-to-the-fire teachers.

In my very first Ayahuasca cycle, she threw multiple books at me in an image, and all I saw was that my name appeared on each and every cover. It took me fifteen years, but here I am, finally honoring this vision. I never would have had the audacity to even consider the books would be about the sacred plants; hence all these years of wild adventures and experiences were needed before I could ink a single word.

Yet I trust I'm right/write on time. And there are no words for how blessed and honored I am to get to share these insights and experiences.

Working as a Guide to the Other Side

I love pouring plant medicine for sincere seekers out to heal and expand. I love it to my absolute core. But it comes with risks and pressures and a level of responsibility I don't have the proper words to articulate. Who knows if there are any such words! Furthermore, there are scads and scads of folks stepping up to take on this role these days; there is no shortage of medicine ceremonies to choose from, and no shortage of folks who want to be shamans, and thus name themselves as such. (We will explore later on in the book how to make sure you land in good hands.)

What isn't as prominent is a focus on integration. It's beginning to become a priority for some, but we are in the infancy of spreading the word about how utterly crucial it is to take the time to integrate peak experiences; from plant medicines, from trauma, from life itself. Along with being a messenger for the plants, my full-time focus is now more about the aftermath than the ceremonies themselves.

In order to have the audacity to write this book, however, I had to own my ability to channel the plants, and to (*gulp*) speak on their behalf. They are alive. They have personalities. They have unlimited power and ridiculously ancient wisdom. But they do not have a voice. I am insanely honored to be one of the humans they use as a messenger.

Because there are many amazing books by intelligent beings out there about the scientific foundations that allow plants like Ayahuasca and Psilocybin to change our mental and physical states, I will not repeat what those much more knowledgeable than I have already gifted the world. Instead, I will give you what the plants themselves have shown me: Who they are in their essence, how they work with us on a spiritual level, and what they want the world to know right now, through me.

My hope is that this gives you a strong educational foundation to find the plants that best align with what you seek for healing and awakening, and that you feel empowered to do so in a safe and effective manner.

Please note that what I share is not Absolute Truth, but the truth as the plants have relayed to me and my best effort to interpret their mind-blowing wisdom. Like us, the plants are so diverse, so infinitely conscious, they can show up for each of us in entirely different ways as they mirror what we need to see and feel in any given moment. That said, they are not one-size-fits-all, and this book will aim to explore who each of these superheroes really is. I can only do my best and don't for a moment pretend to know it all. Only this tiny pixel of wisdom I share with you. But if I do say so myself, it's a luscious little badass pixel. It practically throbs.

Here is what I do know: I am alive and thriving, full of love and gratitude each and every day, and it's all because I once followed my heart and went to the jungle to drink Ayahuasca. Fifteen years later, I want to scream from the rooftops about how incredible plant consciousness is.

Mystery #2: Shamanic Cosmology, or a Slithering Trek Through Consciousness

What I Mean When I Say What I Mean

In order to go on this deeply personal and perilous journey of consciousness together, it's important that we have a shared dialogue of terms like spirit and soul. So first I will share what the plants have taught me about consciousness; specifically the dimension that we exist in, why we're here, the different levels we have access to, and how to make sense of it all; at least, how *I* make sense of it all.

You'll hear/see me reference duality a lot; this is the way in which we all experience our base-level reality. By this I mean, we feel and navigate our perceptions through contrast—gradients. We have dark and light, hot and cold, evil and good, etc. This happens because we have both a mind/ego and a heart; one experiences separateness and the other unity. We are very unique on our planet, as humans are, apparently, the only beings to fully immerse in this separateness.

I asked Ayahuasca once why on Earth she was so invested in assisting humanity to heal and awaken. I was in the jungle, and earlier that day had witnessed multiple logging trucks decimate her plants and wildlife. I couldn't understand why powerful beings like Ayahuasca and Huachuma (an incredible cactus medicine we will merrily explore later on in the book) were so willing to help us in such profound ways.

She told me this: They help us because we are doing the difficult work of making what is unconscious, conscious. We are the ones who feel the horrifying pain of the experience of separation—the symbolic cross we all have to bear. And we are the ones who hold our own fate—and in some ways, the fate of the planet—in our very frightened, often very inept hands. So the plants aim to help us with our Herculean task. And if we all succeed, and the planet deems it so, this incredible space ball we all live on will be around in the same form it is now for gazillions of generations of people—and plants and animals—to enjoy.

It's also very important to note that I unequivocally connect with the eternal energy of our souls. My coaching practice is called AfterLife Coaching; not just because it's clever wordplay, but because I have had the incredible blessing of connecting with consciousness outside of a body—and therefore duality—multiple times. Most of this is thanks to

Mother Ayahuasca, who is famous for giving us the experience of ego death. If we all knew how safe death really was, and if we carried that memory in our conscious awakening, we would be so much kinder to ourselves, each other, and the planet. We wouldn't operate from fear. We would know we are eternal; we literally have all the time in the multiverse to figure this out, and we would know this is a blessed ride to enjoy and soak up, rather than to resist and feel tortured by. My beloved spiritual mentor, Tim Freke, likes to remind us that if we don't wake up every morning in awe of this entire process of being conscious, living in a body, and playing around in Earth School, we aren't truly awake. Consciousness is pure magic. And we. Are. That.

Everything I do, everything I say and write, is rooted in these beliefs, which are factual to me as I have experienced their truths to the point of no longer finding it possible to feign skepticism. I highly encourage discernment and to always bring our skeptics along to any adventure, but mine has nothing to say about the beauty of death, the eternal nature of our souls, and the infinite love of the universe; except to nod in emphatic agreement. We are all just aspects of consciousness experiencing love for itself, and those of us waking up to this magic are truly the lucky ones.

Now, let's talk about the difference between "Spirit" and "Soul." We use these terms interchangeably in our spiritual language, often without a clear understanding of what we mean when we speak each word.

They deserve their own distinctions, as they are each a portal into the deepest aspects of our experience of duality.

I have derived my personal definitions from hundreds of Ayahuasca journeys, years of reading masters like Carl Jung and James Hillman, lots of retreats with folks like Tim Freke and Richard Moss, and my own personal musings. You don't have to agree in the least, but I offer this as a shared dialogue and understanding.

Great Spirit

Let's start with the more playful, unifying, ethereal, delicious aspect of Spirit.

Google's definition of Spirit looks like this:[1]

noun

1. the nonphysical part of a person that is the seat of emotions and character; the soul.

   "we seek a harmony between body and spirit"

   synonyms: soul, psyche, (inner) self, inner being, inner man/woman, mind, ego, id;

2. those qualities regarded as forming the definitive or typical elements in the character of a person, nation, or group or in the thought and attitudes of a particular period.

   "the university is a symbol of the nation's egalitarian spirit"

   synonyms: ethos, prevailing tendency, motivating force, animating principle, essence, quintessence;

verb

3. convey rapidly and secretly.

   "stolen cows were **spirited away** some distance to prevent detection"

---

[1] https://www.google.com/search?q=spirit+definition. As of May 6, 2021

Even the dictionary says that soul and spirit are synonyms. In my heart and mind, they are dance partners, but they are very much like the masculine and the feminine—that is, similar, but not at all the same.

What resonates with the definition above is #2, where spirit is used in connection to the essence of a character or group. It's intangible but has quintessential qualities of speed, excitement, force, mystery, and, as #3 expresses, a secretive nature.

To me, spirit is the essence within us that connects directly to source. When we are connected to spirit, we are in the experience of oneness. Spirit comes rushing out through the crown and straight into the cosmos. It holds deep wisdom of where we come from. I grew up Catholic, and we were all about the Holy Spirit: the essence of life force. I deeply resonate with this truth.

Our spirits are our connection to creation. When we are deep inside spirit, we do not feel disconnected, separate, or individual. I think of spirit as the chariot to the non-dual space. When I surrender into the movement, "I" fall away, and it all feels like We. One. Delicious unity. The magical Noosphere.

It's rare in our language that we personify spirit. We don't normally say, "My spirit." We often drop the pronoun altogether and say, "spirit." *That is the hidden sign that spirit provides direct access to oneness. The holographic god sparks shine within all of us.*

And now for something completely different...

Soul Story

Here is Google's definition of soul:[2]

noun

1. the spiritual or immaterial part of a human being or animal, regarded as immortal.

   synonyms: soul, psyche

2. emotional or intellectual energy or intensity, especially as revealed in a work of art or an artistic performance.

   "their interpretation lacked **soul**"

   synonyms: inspiration, feeling, emotion, passion, animation;

3. the essence or embodiment of a specified quality.

   "he was **the soul of** discretion"

   synonyms: embodiment, personification, incarnation, epitome, quintessence, essence;

Like spirit, soul has synonyms like essence and epitome. What works above is defining soul as immortal, and the embodiment of incarnation.

For me, soul is the opposite of spirit in many ways. Soul is like our energetic snowflake. It's the part of us that is unique in all of creation. When we say something is soulful, we normally mean that it's *deep*. Intense. Full of feeling. Intangible. And we often refer to it in a creative context.

---

[2] https://www.google.com/search?q=soul+definition&oq=soul. As of June 21, 2021.

Inside the seat of the soul is the full experience of separateness. That's why we don't call the intense moments, "dark nights of the spirit." They are aptly named "dark nights of the soul."

While spirit shoots out into the cosmos, soul goes down into the core.

Soul dares to deep dive into the darkness. We actualize the truth of our souls by having the courage to know our shadow.

Carl Jung put it this way:

> *By soul...I understand a clearly demarcated functional complex that can best be described as a "personality."*[3]

I love this description, because it's been my experience that the more we get to know the true essence of our souls, the more we know who we are as authentic individuals.

James Hillman talked about the soul as an acorn: Within the soul is the entire spectrum of our individual potential. The soul holds the oak tree of our human expression. The more we go in, learn, ask, feel, and integrate, the more we are able to live in the truth of who we are and what we came to do.[4]

Soul emerges into our beingness through the root chakra, the opposite of spirit. It moves up into our awareness only after we go to greet it in the darkness. As we make soul conscious, we become aligned with who we really are.

Spirit manifests the masculine force, akin to Prana in Hindu tradition; that is, the life force that, like a lightning bolt, comes down from the

---

[3] C. G. Jung (1921) *Psychological Types, The Collected Works of C. G. Jung,* Vol. 6, par. 797, Princeton, NJ: Bollingen—Princeton University Press.
[4] James Hillman (1997) *The Soul's Code: In Search of Character and Calling.*

heavens and animates, electrifies, and illuminates our conscious experience.

In contrast, soul is the feminine force, the Akasha; she dwells in the core of darkness, awaiting our union, which happens through awareness and love.

Spirit gives us the energy and motivation to find our way to soul. We have to courageously journey through our shadow to fully meet our souls, which is why the darkest events of our lives teach us the most about who we are.

They are one hell of a dynamic duo.

Spirit + Soul − Body = Liberation

Here's where two become one…

It is my experience, through a lifelong study of death and through my own near-death experience (NDE) journeys, that spirit and soul are only separate while we live in duality. Because everything here has contrast, we can consciously experience both as separate energies.

When we die, we simply remove our consciousness from the confinements of a body. We step out of the density of duality and back into the freedom of unity.

Through that, spirit and soul merge once the body is dropped. This is why we use the terms interchangeably—when we're talking about interacting with beings that have passed on, they are both souls and spirits, as those are the immortal parts of who we are.

And this explains why they do work as synonyms for each other; both are aspects of each other.

But here, while we are blessed (and offered the thrilling and delicious challenge) with the dualistic journey of living in a body, spirit and soul have vastly different roles. They provide the experience of contrast.

How ridiculously lucky we are to get to know both the unified and separated essences of our unique swirl of consciousness. We are, each one of us, a one-of-a-kind embodiment of spiritual soulfulness.

Where Is Here, and Why Am I There?

Now, here's the big question that always comes up when any of us has a true existential crisis; if we are very lucky and curious, with a zest for life, we eventually get to wondering why the bejeezus we are here at all.

If nothing means what we thought it meant, if we're eternal and death is a lie, why go through this intensity over and over again?

Because we can! Life is available, and it's the only game in town. What consciousness cares about is growth. We are always expanding. The multiverse is so ridiculously vast and mysterious that, the truth is, we know very little about how it all came to be and where it's all going. But we do know we experience things. We feel. Deeply. And that is precisely what we came here to do.

Each one of us is an aspect of the absolute. Source woke up one morning and thought, I would like to experience myself in a wholly unique way. I will create that crazy wonderful being right there.

And so it is.

We are here for the whole damn spectrum of experience. Heartbreak and loss, terror and pain, bliss and joy, and most of all, for love. Real love–the unconditional, mind-blowing variety that, when you feel it, helps you to know that you were never disconnected from source/God/the universe, that all you are is love, and that every single moment of every single one of your lives was meant to help you remember this.

Now, why do we come in forgetting our eternal nature, the story of our soul in our lives before—the truth of who we are?

Because if we remembered, we would have zero motivation to keep expanding. If we didn't have the experience of contrast—the very real fear that death was the ending—we wouldn't have the urgency to continue growing. We grow through suffering just as much as we do through love and happiness. Maybe more. Maybe that's why there's such a seemingly endless stream of suffering on our beautiful planet. It's pretty obvious humanity has a lot to learn. And all of it matters to consciousness—which is why it all exists. There are no mistakes.

Before I dive head first into all the many ways in which psychedelic plants help us to awaken, heal, and return to love, I first want to take us to the dark side. That's where the healing happens, and if you work with any of these plants long enough, they will take you to your own version of hell, when you're ready and lucky enough to get a round trip ticket.

The Current Necessity of Violence and Suffering

It's a natural inclination to start pondering how and why things like mass shootings, war, and all the various ways we enact violence against each other has to exist. Who on earth could cause death and destruction intentionally to a fellow human; or worse still, thousands of fellow beings?

What could the motive be?

To really understand how all this could occur, we have to look within.

Every murderer has their own individual story and reasons for causing harm to another being, but I can promise it comes from one core issue: Pain. Deep, soul-ripping, mind-numbing pain.

Crime = cry + me

In no way am I justifying the actions of anyone who chooses to cause harm. But this tendency we have to want to label anyone "evil" or "monstrous" isn't helpful, true, or in any way healing. Their actions may be monstrous, but they are human. They are us.

We are all made of the same consciousness. Some of us shield immense trauma and use that to motivate us to be more compassionate and loving. Others experience a normal life yet spiral into anger and depression, and a select few of us will go forth and commit heinous crimes. The whole probability distribution manifests, sinners and saints.

There is no formula of prediction, no handbook of horror. We desperately want to dissect the psyche of every killer so that we can feel safe in predicting the next psychopathic event. But it will never work that way. Darkness doesn't wear a uniform. Darkness looks like you and me.

As difficult as it is to process, we will never be able to predict who among us will ultimately snap and cause harm. This is not a game of detective work, criminal profiling, or even understanding psychology.

But there is a way to crack this code.

When we divide people into "good" and "bad" categories, we create a tremendous disservice in that separation. We deny ourselves the opportunity to really understand the force that causes the worst events in our world.

If you desire to understand what causes someone to shoot and murder another being, spend all the time you can getting to know the pain you hold inside your heart. Although we say that pain is relative, it is also universal. The force that causes someone to commit suicide is the same one that propels an act of violence externally, too. It's also the same force that drives millions of people to gobble anti-depressants, causes untold numbers of anxiety attacks, and affects everyone on one level or another.

There is a killer and a saint inside each one of us. The more we are willing to actually recognize and feel that energy, rather than deny and fight with it, the more we are likely to be part of the love in this world.

Making Darkness Your BFF

It's not the darkness that causes us to snap and lash out. It's our relationship with it.

I love to call that untamed space we spend most of our lives trying to avoid inside ourselves the "darkness." I adore that term because it's impersonal, and does not directly imply evil or goodness. Darkness is neutral. It's just a space absent of light.

So how is it the force that causes rape, murder, and madness?

In truth, that space is not responsible. We are. Our relationship to the energies within is what creates the actions that result.

Conflict manifests when resistance appears. And resistance generates fear. If we agree to feel the trauma and hurt we carry, we are not in conflict with it. That doesn't make it easy or fun in any way to feel, but it does make it healing when we say "yes" to those emotions.

I am not immune to horrific bouts of darkness. I have obsessed over pondering suicide, been wildly self-destructive, and have had trips into depression that felt as if they would certainly destroy me.

I am still the same person with all the same intensities now, but I no longer am motivated to harm myself or others. It's not that I only feel loving or happy emotions now–quite the contrary. The only difference is that I know how to cease fighting with my shadow. When the pain comes in, I meet it with compassion and reverence, as best I can. I give it my all to feel those energies and let them in with my whole heart. The result is poetic: When I welcome my own emotions, it is then effortless to honor everyone else's pain. I say yes to what is. And that makes all the difference.

The good news is that the universe is always, always in balance. That's what the universe *is*.

I lived in Vegas during the mass shooting that occurred against the crowd of a country music festival in 2017. The day after the horrific event occurred, I literally couldn't find a place to give blood because the lines stretched around city blocks with generous souls wanting to support the injured. Discussion boards and social media were teeming with volunteers willing to do just about anything to help. People were softer, kinder, more in their hearts–wherever you went in the city–for weeks and weeks after. I was so humbled by the compassion we are all capable of expressing. I yearn for the time when this is our natural state of being.

I can promise you that anyone who has ever gone on a killing spree didn't feel heard, cared for, or nurtured in this world. They hurt others because they hurt inside themselves. They develop disdain and hatred for a world they feel alienated from, and they depersonalize the people they end up hurting.

Compassion cuts through that animosity with a burst of healing light. Every single time we show love and empathy to someone, we break down their walls of destruction.

By contrast, every time we judge someone, hurl insults or nastiness, we build up the dam of darkness inside them.

This doesn't mean we are all to blame when someone goes rogue and lashes out. It does mean we are empowered to do our part to prevent future disasters.

The solution is simple to describe, but unbelievably complex to execute. This was a direct download from Ayahuasca the weekend after the Vegas shootings, when I went to her with a broken heart and a desire to be a part of the solution.

Here's what she told me:

1) Make it your mission to know, feel, and integrate your shadow. Do not run from or resist those painful emotions inside of you; make friends with them instead. Feel them with your whole heart. Tell trusted loved ones what is going on within. Be real about your feelings. Let them pass through you and be free.

2) The more you show that love and compassion for yourself, the more you will effortlessly give it to everyone you meet.

Like attracts like. The more we feel love, the more we give love, the more we receive love.

Of course, the reverse is true too.

It turns out that in order to give social distance to the darkness, we first have to honor, to feel it, and to move through it.

She told me that when we each consciously decide what kind of world we want to live in, and do our best to show up in that space in every moment, we can literally transform it. We don't have to be perfect or graceful at this; just honest. Just real, transparent, and raw.

Let's not wait for Congress to pass gun laws that create a false sense of safety. Let's keep being compassionate and loving and gentle with each other. In that space, guns don't matter.

People who love people don't hurt people. More of that, please.

Life on Earth, In the Now

Although there are still some wildly ignorant naysayers, it's painfully obvious to the vast majority of us that Pachamama will not be able to sustain the level of abuse and toxicity we are unleashing on her for much longer. And while there are many beautiful activists out there fighting to save the planet, I'm of the opinion that she's not the one that needs saving: We are.

If we continue pumping noxious gases into her atmosphere, raping her soil of nutrients, killing off countless species of plants and animals, and burning down her forests and jungles, she will continue to transform. She has morphed into different versions of herself for billions of years. We aren't powerful enough to force her to disappear.

She, however, is powerful enough to make *us* disappear. And that is the cause we are truly working towards avoiding if we are to align with her.

The year 2020 was a big dose of humble pie reflecting this truth. The fires, the hurricane and storms, the temperature shifts, and that global, world-changing pandemic—all the extremes she showed us; that's our planet in distress. Her warning signs are getting louder.

This is the urgency that has propelled me to write this book, in truth. I don't think I'm being dramatic when I say I feel the possibility that we are nearing the point of no return. It's even possible we've passed it, but I don't operate in negativity; I operate in the trust that every single one of us that wakes up and commits to living in harmony with nature, instead of destruction, helps us take one step closer to ensure we have this beautiful planet for thousands of lifetimes to come.

After fifteen years of working with plant consciousness, I unequivocally have felt this urgency fester and rise. As I write this, the Amazon is burning,[5] California is burning,[6] Colorado is burning,[7] Mexico is about to be buried by a category 5 hurricane,[8] a million species of animals are predicted to be extinct in the next decade,[9] each and every month is noted as the hottest one on record,[10] and governments around the world are refusing to acknowledge that climate change is even an issue.[11]

The psychotropic plants care very much about this continuous downward trend; they like living here too. It's up to the human population to determine which direction this will go. And so they are very much engaged in helping us awaken and to support us in the task

---

[5] https://www.greenpeace.org/international/story/44159/fires-brazil-bolsonaro-amazon-deforestation-2020

[6] https://www.fire.ca.gov/incidents/2020

[7] https://www.nbcnews.com/news/us-news/3-largest-wildfires-colorado-history-have-occurred-2020-n1244525

[8]https://www.washingtonpost.com/weather/2020/10/12/hurricane-delta-winds-surge-rain

[9] https://www.cnn.com/2020/01/14/world/un-biodiversity-draft-plan-intl-hnk-scli-scn/index.html

[10] https://www.ncdc.noaa.gov/sotc/global/202011

[11]https://www.nytimes.com/interactive/projects/cp/climate/2015-paris-climate-talks/where-in-the-world-is-climate-denial-most-prevalent

of coming home to our hearts so that we all have the opportunity to call Earth our home for eons to come.

It's a very, very critical time. Which means it's ridiculously awesome to be alive.

Your Grandma Wants to Try Psychedelics

When I first found Ayahuasca and plant medicines, absolutely no one else in my tribe had ever heard of these, let alone journeyed, aside from my man Rocket, the angel who led me to the Amazon that first time. LSD, MDMA, and similar substances were still vilified as recreational drugs with little to no therapeutic merit, and were only accepted in party scenes.

Fast forward a decade and a half, and people from all walks of life are contacting me about where they can safely experience Ayahuasca, Iboga, Huachuma, Psilocybin, and the rest of the entheogenic tribe. I have sat with grandmothers who had never had a sip of alcohol, UFC fighters looking to understand their anger and sharpen their focus, addicts struggling to find meaning and the power to survive, poker players looking to hone their instincts, people with every conceivable illness and disorder, young twenty-somethings wanting to know more about consciousness, and people on the last chapter of their lives making friends with death; it's really a limitless list of the types of folks who are stepping forth to know the mysteries of these portals.

People are ultimately waking up to the fact that the Western, allopathic method of health care, at least in the United States, is driven by profits, not healing. More and more, we are becoming aware that the pharmaceutical companies have been running the show, and now that they are being held legally accountable for the opioid epidemic,[12] we are really feeling the waves of awakening for the masses. This comes with tremendous pain that the system so many have trusted to take care of us hasn't done so at all; quite the contrary. But it has also triggered enormous empowerment that we each are taking our health and well-being into our own hands. That's where it has always belonged, so this was just a matter of time.

Then came the COVID-19 pandemic, all the misinformation, the confusion and the chaos; it's clear no one really knows the secrets to healthy living, mainly because it has never been one-size-fits-all. So know that if you have a desire to heal yourself, to let go of disease, anxiety, pain, and trauma, and to reconnect with the force of love, you aren't doing this as an act of selfishness. Not only do we, as individuals, reap the benefits of doing the work to heal and wake up to the loving beings we really are, our friends and family get to witness and experience the positive effects, and the whole world also experiences the positive shift of this beautiful work. If we want to continue to enjoy this incredible planet and the existence she offers, I suggest we all find an Ayahuasca circle, stat.

---

[12] https://sbtreatment.com/blog/purdue-pharma-settlement

Testimony #2: Rebekah Shaman

Plant Medicine Facilitator, Managing Director of the British Hemp Alliance

The most important thing the plant medicines taught me was that I am a part of this wondrous eco-system, not apart from it, and what I do to myself, I am doing to the earth, and what I do to the earth, I am doing to myself. There is no separation—we are one and the same. They transformed my separation consciousness, to unity consciousness.

They fundamentally changed me by helping me to love myself in order to love Mother Earth and all her inhabitants. By showing me the selfish ego illusion I had of myself, I was able to shift my consciousness. Only when I began truly loving myself did I know that I was also Mother Earth. That is what unity consciousness is all about. Once I knew this, I had a mission—to live this unity consciousness, and help to bring humanity and the environment back into balance.

Mother Earth is a living organism, and the plant medicines are desperate for us to wake up and realise we are destroying our home. We are at a point in history when we desperately need to consciously remember that we are a *part* of nature. The plant medicines showed me that humanity's only real purpose is to leave this planet healthy and thriving for future generations. If we don't look after the planet that is looking after us, we are going to become extinct.

It is going to take a shift in consciousness, and a value system reset, to bring humanity and the planet back into balance. We need to reawaken our right brains, so that we can access empathic, compassionate, and intuitive thinking, and come into unity consciousness.

Plant Medicines reawaken the right side of the brain. They show us that we are part of this delicate web of life and that all life is sacred. They are vital for our evolutionary growth, as they help us shift our values and principles to protect and support life, and realign us, once again, with the Anima Mundi (Spirit of the World).

Instead, of our behaviour being solely for personal gain, we understand that even our smallest actions affect the whole, including politically (with our vote), economically (with our buying decisions), ecologically (with our lifestyle decisions), abundantly (with our giving decisions), and emotionally (with our attitude towards ourselves and others).

Plant medicines are so important, as they are sparking this next step in humanity's evolution. We are seeing a global explosion of their uses because they unlock the right side of the brain, transforming separation consciousness into unity consciousness, and automatically shifting our value systems, so we preserve and sustain a thriving and healthy planet for all living things for the next seven generations.

Rebekah Shaman
www.rebekahshaman.com

Mystery #3: Altered State Omnipotence: Lessons Learned

Why Should We Seek to Change Our Reality?

Why is it that altering our consciousness equates to an experience that can be healing and expansive? Why isn't it just fun times on drugs?

In very simple terms, altering our consciousness allows us to feel and experience ourselves and the world in a much different frame of reference, and that alone can bring about the kind of insight that shifts a perspective and lifts us out of misery.

If a person suffers from depression, doing the same things repeatedly that created the experience of darkness will only bring about more sadness. We know if we're stuck in a rut of any sort, we have to mix it up. Change of any kind is required to move the energy.

And what does the mind resist the most? Change. Because our minds adore the idea of security, they will do just about anything to prevent us from creating any form of transformation. This is because the mind naturally fears the unknown, and this fear makes us assume change will be negative, and it keeps many of us stagnant for months, years, even lifetimes.

Fundamentally, that which the mind seeks to know is, in fact, unknowable—we cannot mentally comprehend the truth of who we are, our power, our eternal nature, our endless portals of love. So instead, the mind stays attached to what it *can* know: Suffering.

Repeating the same patterns and behaviors that created any state of suffering we are facing; that's the real enemy. Change is the angel that can usher us into a higher state of being.

I had a spiritual teacher that used to say a spiritual shift happens because one of the four "C's" has occurred. These are:

1) Clinical: A near-death experience, a brush with illness or an accident that makes us question our mortality; these are highly effective ways that we change our perceptions and learn more about who we are.

2) Cultural: This category covers the many different rituals and habits that different religions and cultures have adapted in

order to create a shift of consciousness. Cultural actions that bring about change include meditation, chanting, yoga (the real kind, not the yoga that simply focuses on burning calories), sound healing, etc.

3) Crisis: The recent pandemic and the resulting fear is a force that helps us awaken and shift our perspective. Addiction, abuse, trauma, and any form of emotional intensity has the same potentiality.

4) Chemical: Altering your state of mind with a plant medicine or psychedelic; also known as The Fast Track.

Working with psychotropic substances is tricky because we have to be both ready for this shift of awareness, without knowing what that will look and feel like, and in the right set and setting so that we don't actually add to our confusion and trauma. "Psychotropic" literally references a substance that alters the mind or mental agencies; therefore it becomes obvious why a mind that adores the safety of sameness would rail against the opportunity to transform.

It stands to reason that the most potent possibilities entail the responsibility of us, the journeyers, to apply humility, respect and discernment into every choice we make.

These amazing substances have been utterly vilified in our culture, at different times and ways, for thousands of years. Why? Because they are so wildly powerful. And the more we work with them responsibly, the more we wake up to the efforts of our Powers that Be to control and manipulate us.

Hence the fight for legality in this nation and many others. Psychedelics have been at times written off as hippie-dippie drugs for anti-establishment types that just want to get high and check out. The fear of altered spaces from those who seek to control the masses has always been more about the immense freedom they allow us to tap into, not the purported dangers that are often emphasized. Society is easier to control when the prevalent emotion is fear; psychedelics help us break out of fear-based mentality, and bring in genuine autonomy. That's implicitly terrifying to governments that want consumerism and obedience to reign supreme.

Now, our culture faces another massive uptick in awareness of the therapeutic powers of psychotropics, and those of us on the front lines are holding the intent that we do so with reverence, caution, groundedness, and safety. Past generations have laid the groundwork for this movement; it's all happening in divine timing. Keeping a reverent awareness of the sacredness of the substances, as well as the precious lessons of the past, creates the opportunity for our present-day movement to grow and grow and grow. But we cannot do so by ignoring the beautiful Pandora's box that psychedelics necessarily rip open.

Without a doubt, it is our birthright to have access to any option we choose for indelible change, and we can see that evidence in every facet of our existence right now. We are in a time of incredible shadow exploration on the most personal and mass conscious levels. We are witnessing so much of the once-latent misogyny, racism, religious profiling, homophobia, and hatred against those who dare to alter their physical sex. Notice the theme of where the hatred is directed? To the "other," however that is currently defined. Consciousness is dynamic, yet egos fear the flow of change. Yet that fear can never change the fact that we are all sovereign beings with the sacred right to be who we are.

If you read or watch the news, it feels as though the world is in complete chaos, and many feel hopeless as a result. The plants have taught me this is all actually very, very good news; just as looking at our individual subconscious is priceless in our own growth and healing, so it is true for us on a cultural level. All of these judgments, fears, and emotions have been hidden beneath the surface of humanity for a long time, and this is just another wave of bringing all this darkness to light. We absolutely have to encounter and *be with* these shadowy prejudices and traumas so that we can move forward in a higher state of consciousness.

It's happening. And the surge of popularity in the usage of psychedelics from people of all walks of life is one of the many signs that point to a positive outcome. Millions of us are doing the work to heal the edges in our psyche that cause violence, self-sabotage, anger, and profiling. That is undoubtedly leading us to a brighter place in our cultural development. We're in the *breakdown* right now, but the *breakthrough* is coming. It's not a matter of *if*, but *when*.

No Trip to Heaven Can Bypass Hell

I've dropped the "shadow work" phrase a few times in this book so far, so let's do a deep dive to define this as it's integral to the process of working with plant medicine and psychedelics.

In very simple terms, shadow work is looking into the part of your consciousness that you were previously unaware of. Whenever we hold the intention to do any psychological or spiritual work that exposes new information about ourselves and the universe, we are doing shadow work.

Most people relate this term to the exploration of our darkness: the source of suffering, self-sabotage, and sadness. Yes, shadow work often involves the willingness to look at, feel, and process our pain. This is the pain that has derived from our experience of separateness. Because we humans are lucky enough to have the capacity for self-reflection, we can also fall for the mirage created by that reflection, and we are granted the experience of feeling disconnected from the world, ourselves and each other. And that is the source of all suffering.

Many of us have done the work to begin to intellectually understand that this sense of separation is actually false because we are all connected and all born from the same God/source/universal energy. But if all we do is intellectually grasp this concept, we are not actually vibrating in this truth; it remains a thought rather than an experience.

To feel the truth of anything, we have to first traverse the shadow of it. That is the gift of duality.

This means that to truly know and feel the truth of our connectedness, our Godliness, our incredible vibration of love, we must first feel and experience the opposite of all those beautiful frequencies. Depression, disconnectedness, alienation, and apathy are all contrasting emotions from those we seek to experience, but it's important to know that when we feel any of these shadowy energies, we are right where we need to be.

We are so programmed in our Western world to whole-heartedly believe that if we are suffering, if we are prone to darkness and rage and fear, we are broken. Nothing could be further from the truth. Those states of consciousness are available, and that's why we are privileged to visit them. It can certainly seem at times that some folks drew the short straw and have way more than their share of curveballs and pain points; that's true if we look at the microcosm of a handful of years, but it isn't true when we view the Big Picture. Every hero's journey involves trips to hell. When we go there, it is simply our turn. And it's an *honor,* if we may say so. Profound learning and expansion await in the shadows. And despite the convincing feelings that such spaces are permanent, we are always just passing through.

If you consider that everything is always in balance, the degree to which we feel the intensity of darkness will at some point be in complete balance with the degree to which we feel love and joy. We don't know when that will occur, but it's coming.

Every myth, every hero's journey, every story of empowerment has a sacred experience of hell—or two or three or dozens. Heaven and hell are states of consciousness, the ultimate expression of duality, so if we want to know what it feels like to be in a true state of unconditional love for all, we first visit the hellish experience of complete breakdown, aloneness, and terrible suffering.

Knowing that this is the journey of all conscious beings helps tremendously to trust the darkness when it comes swooping in to visit. And swoop in it will. We are never being tortured by the universe when we suffer, we are being expanded and taught how to be powerful enough to welcome and embrace that experience—all experiences. Suffering helps make us conscious. It is just as divine and sacred as love.

Yet there's a much more exciting and positive aspect to our shadow, one Jung called the Golden Shadow.[13] This is the unconscious part of ourselves that holds the entirety of our potential. Your Golden Shadow holds your untapped powers, talents, and gifts. It is the infinite part of you waiting to be discovered, so that you can step into a full, authentic version of yourself.

---

[13] https://www.melanieryanlcsw.com/jung-shadow

Shadow does not imply bad or negative. Just hidden. If we adopt a joyful view of discovery, every moment of this work is a blessing.

This is all very relevant to a discussion about the usage of psychedelics, as each and every one of them can help to intensify any experience of duality. Use them long enough, and you will visit your own personal version of hell, and heaven, likely multiple times, as an invitation to learn to love all of it. The darkest nights on these offerings bring the most transformative lessons. Once again, everything is always in balance. I will talk more about navigating a dark night of the soul on these medicines later on, but just know that choosing to work with psychedelics means you are granting yourself the opportunity to know about the entire spectrum of consciousness. You cannot control these journeys and insist on only visiting the light, just like you can't ask life to deny you the opportunity to suffer. So you have full disclosure that psychedelics take you into the unknown, the untamed spaces, and anything and everything isn't just possible, it's guaranteed.

The Many Faces of Shamanism

Everyone has heard the terms "shamanism" and "shaman," but what do they really mean?

That's an answer that is as personal as the journey itself.

Fundamentally, shamanism is defined as a religious, ritualistic practice involving a mergence of the physical and spiritual worlds. The word "shaman" is originally from Siberia, and one of the definitions that seems most appropriate is that it means "one who sees in the dark." This is my preferred explanation as this is the perfect summary of the experience I have when I'm walking this path.

Ayahuasca once gave me this vision and metaphor: A shaman is just another human being in the cave of duality, seeking the light with all the other tribe members. The only difference is the medicine men and women have a hat with a light on. They are the ones in the community that help guide the whole tribe out of the darkness, out of suffering, and back into the space of feeling healthy and whole. That image always makes my heart happy.

There are shamanistic rituals in indigenous cultures throughout the world, including all parts of Asia, South America, Europe, Scandinavia, and within Native American tribes. In all cases, a deep connection to nature and spirit are the calling cards of the shaman. There are different intricacies and tools used for every tribe, but each one honors the power of the Earth as the primary partner to heal and awaken.

In order to lift the veil and have a conscious awareness of the spiritual world while we dwell in the tangible space of duality, some form of ritual is almost always necessary. These rituals might involve meditation, chanting, drumming, and of course, the usage of powerful plant medicines to alter our default reality.

The shaman then, otherwise known as the medicine man or woman, is the conductor of the rituals, the captain of the spaceship, and they are responsible for guiding their brothers and sisters safely through the wild curves of consciousness.

In my training, I have been lucky enough to deeply experience the Shipibo-Conibo lineage of Ayahuasca, which is a tribe in the wildly magical Amazon jungle. I have also studied the Chavin culture, a tribe of people that lived far up in the Peruvian Andes, and who are sometimes considered the godfathers of Huachuma shamanism.

Did you know Peru has more temple and pyramid ruins than Egypt? And that many archaeologists and historians believe there was a link between the rituals and knowledge of Egypt and Peru?[14] We don't know for sure, but what is certain is that Peru's history is rich with the sacred usage of various powerful plant medicines, and there are many temples ("huacas" in Quechua[15]) that still remain throughout this diverse nation, and some are even accessible to tourists.

Hello Neo-Shamanism. It's Nice to Meet You?

The shamanic arts are experiencing a massive renaissance, for all the reasons I've mentioned so far and many more. It would seem our Western culture has vagabonded so far into the space of individualism, capitalism, and religion, that we've started to awaken to the awareness that these perspectives are limiting. Separation creates suffering, which creates illness and mental breakdown. A return to the shamanic path is one vital way we can attain balance.

Just a handful of decades ago, even the indigenous people did not always partake in any of the psychotropic medicines they revered. Instead, they would sit with the resident shaman (male or female), who would work with the plants, journey, and return with information, tools, or various rituals to help heal and awaken their patients. It was only with the arrival of the Westerners in the 60s that the participants themselves started to join the shaman in consuming the plants, and we've been off to the races ever since.

---

[14] https://adeptinitiates.com/from-egypt-to-peru and the works of Stephen Mehler, https://stephenmehler.wordpress.com

[15] The Quechua are a South American people of Peru and parts of Bolivia, Chile, Columbia, and Ecuador. The language they speak is also "Quechua."

Shamanism was an immediate draw for me because it cuts out the middleman. I grew up Catholic, and I always inherently objected to the notion that only a priest could create a bridge between myself and divine energy. Working with plants like Ayahuasca and Huachuma allow us, as individuals, to touch the purest parts of consciousness without needing someone else to transmute. The shaman conducts and holds space, and the trifecta of the facilitator, the medicine, and the journeyer create the partnership that literally allows magic to unfold. This is part of many ancient traditions based on self-knowledge or "gnosis."

There are many tricky elements to the continued spread of everyday people using psychedelics, however, and this book will explore many of them. Logistically speaking, the most obvious hurdle that currently exists is the legal one. Laws are changing rapidly worldwide, but as I write this only a handful of countries have legalized and/or decriminalized plant medicines,[16,17] while many more are investigating similar legislation.

In the U.S., the recent legalization in many states of Cannabis is fantastically encouraging, and cities like Oakland and Denver have followed suit to decriminalize substances like Psilocybin and DMT.[18] There is still a very long battle to legitimize the usage of all plant medicines and allow everyone safe and legal access, but if you had asked me a handful of years ago if we'd be at the place we are now, I would have been highly skeptical. Instead, now I'm highly encouraged. I have decided to write this book in part because I want to support the

---

[16] https://en.wikipedia.org/wiki/Drug_liberalization
[17] https://en.wikipedia.org/wiki/Legal_status_of_ayahuasca_by_country
[18] https://www.denverpost.com/2019/06/05/oakland-magic-mushroom-decriminalization/

movement of legalization, but to also ask that we bring these plants to the mainstream with reverence, intelligence, safety, and love.

The legal hurdles don't prevent the plants from spreading through the underground, but facilitators should not have to risk their freedom in order to carry these medicines to sincere seekers looking to feel better in their bodies, minds, and spirits. I am holding the vision that in my lifetime this risk will be nullified and/or eradicated, and that plant medicines will be available to anyone who wishes to use them responsibly. How does one hold a vision in this manner? By leaning in to how it will feel when this is manifested, as if it already has. Then the universe has no choice but to acquiesce.

There's obviously endless debates and challenges around this topic, some of which I will cover later on, but let's at least take this moment to celebrate the progress that has been made, and vow to continue this mission in a grounded, respectful, and dedicated manner. With every new person that awakens to the awareness that it is their birthright to alter their consciousness in any way they see fit, the movement is strengthened, and we are one step closer to the system supporting us. Soon, it will have no choice. We are omnipotent when we align as a tribe.

Should White People Be Allowed to Carry Out Indigenous Ceremonies?

This is a very, very big topic, and it's obviously near and dear to me as I am white woman who leads old school, authentic shamanic ceremonies. So what follows is clearly my opinion and experience, but my hope is this adds intelligently to this essential debate.

I'll admit that when I first got the strong calling to pursue the path of a shaman, I was riddled with one major concern:

Can a white woman from Montana pour Ayahuasca?

The more I fought the urge, the more Ayahuasca haunted me. I thought of very little else other than a life devoted to plants. I had a tremendous amount of fear around even the idea of pouring a single cup of medicine and what the path would require, but I felt completely consumed with the possibilities.

My genius mind (or was it a genius heart?) conjured up a safe way to compromise; I decided to be an organizer and hostess of ceremonies. That felt grand—I could welcome her and an incredible sha-person into my home on the regular, watching the magic unfold for myself and my tribe, all while owning my power as a master networker and connector of awesome peeps.

The plan worked like a charm—kind of. I hosted ceremonies on the regular. I drank for free and met incredible people. I sat with gifted facilitators and did everything before and after ceremony, with only the requirement of doing my own work and helping on the sidelines during the actual soiree. Crafty, no?

I called myself the Vanna White of shamanism. Da-ding (hands outstretched)—look everyone, a SHAMAN!

Only I still couldn't dodge the dream of going deeper with her.

And then one day I sat in this amazing Shipibo Maestro's ceremony. Within 15 seconds of hearing him sing, I knew I was meant to work with him.

An apprenticeship was born that day. I had every right to be utterly terrified, as this path as a medicine woman—specifically as an

Ayahuasquera—has been devastatingly challenging. And mind-blowingly magical.

Yet there remains a truth I can never shake, nor hide from: My body and physical lineage do not match the traditions I practice every day. Without outside influences, I would never deem this as an issue, for it's so innate and authentic inside me, yet I hear now and then from those that disagree. This disagreement or cultural blockage presents itself, like any other shamanic challenge, as an opportunity and even obligation to grow by working with the energy and its blockage.

So let's explore this. Is it really advantageous that Westerners step up as sacred medicine practitioners?

There's a lot of fire around the audacity of so-called white privileged peeps stepping up and taking ownership of carrying an indigenous lineage. I deeply understand this conundrum. Indeed, in some ways I *am* this conundrum. I battled it so much in my own self-worth that I delayed honoring my calling for years. It was the medicine that encouraged me to pursue this, and she taught me a couple of core things.

First of all, I took an oath with her and my Maestro that I would honor the lineage to the best of my ability; that I would put the medicine and the gift of being her carrier above all other aspects of my life. I've given up a marriage, a years-long career, a consistent source of income, and an overall sense of real-world safety for this path. I've given up normalcy in every sense. It's also dangerous to do what I do, and to speak out about it, because it is not accepted by the powers that be. It's not a stretch to say my freedom is at stake every day.

Most importantly, I am extremely reverent and respectful to the fact that I am so unspeakably blessed to be a medicine carrier. I have never forgotten that she chose me, and as long as that invitation stays, I'm all-in to being her protector.

She's taught me that doing my best is enough. Holding this reverence and sacredness in every ceremony keeps me safe, and protects the lineage I carry. She also undeniably uplifts everything about me that is unique. She uses every gift, every aspect of my shadow—ALL of me—to do this work. There is nothing about me she would change. I know that unequivocally. This is why she is such a perfect Mother.

I am also extraordinarily mindful of the plants and humans that have been guardians of these traditions for thousands of years, and I donate a portion of every single event I lead to the protection and sustainability of Aya and her tribes. I also lead a group of plant medicine folks dedicated to equality in the medicine space, making sure that historically disenfranchised people in our world have equal access to medicine circles. Diversity and inclusion are a very sincere passion. I own the privilege my skin color reflects, and I will never stop doing my part to create balance and fairness.

Above all, I have learned that the sacred medicines we work with are the ones in charge. They choose us. And they are color blind. They create partnerships with our souls, not our DNA. She has assured me I have lived the life of an indigenous being many times over; this time Montana won out as my soul's first home. Why? Because it was exactly where I needed to be.

When I went to her in ceremony ready to humbly accept her offering, she just waved a flag—with an image of the Earth. That's our nationality—earthlings. Everything else is division.

(And then she lined up a seemingly endless stream of medicine men and women from every conceivable tradition and dimension that were both welcoming me and also giving me that "Do you know what you just agreed to oh my god girl hold on to your pigtails" look.)

That said, it's not OK for any of us to dismiss the importance of understanding and respecting the lineage we carry just because we feel chosen. I am constantly a student of all who came before me. I still have mentors and elders who generously teach me ancient wisdom. I have a lot to learn still, and always will, but I'm damn glad I didn't let my birth heritage scare me away from following my soul's path.

Here's the biggest argument for why I finally surrendered into a space of acceptance with my skin color and my path: My teachers embrace me for all that I am, too.

My teacher's teacher is a Shipibo Vegetalista who is one of the pioneers that chose to pass along these traditions to people of all races and lineages. He recognized that the Western world needed Ayahuasca's assistance so much more than the indigenous cultures, and therefore knew in his heart it was the plant's wishes to teach people of all races how to work with her. It's because of his courage that I am blessed to walk this path, and I will never ever be able to properly express my gratitude. But I will certainly keep trying!

When I first met, in ceremony, the man who would become my teacher, I knew within fifteen seconds of hearing his icaros that he was the one to show me the way. When I expressed this post-ceremony, he laughed and called me a bimbo—he was sure I couldn't hack it and dismissed me. Since that wasn't the first time a man misjudged my outward persona, I didn't take it personally, but I gave up the notion that he would ever take me on as a student. But that wasn't the end of the story.

A few months later, this Maestro called me, stating that Ayahuasca kept saying my name. He planted the seed during that phone call that I might have the opportunity to train with him; an honor I knew dozens, if not hundreds, of people were desiring.

I will admit that I still had a very strong urge to run from this calling. To be real, I still battle this urge at times: the fear of the responsibility, the intensity, the danger, the constant shadow work. But then someone shared a book on shamanism with me; it fell open to a page about the repercussions of denying a partnership with a plant spirit who has claimed you. If the plants know you have a soul contract with them and you spend your life avoiding it, misery will prevail.

I felt this in my very core.

And so, I surrendered.

Because the teacher manifested, and the medicine keeps finding me, I know it is her will. She doesn't care about my skin color, my gender, my physical DNA. She cares about the commitment we have to each other. She cares that I own my integrity and never give up the necessity to do my own shadow work. She cares that I serve her, with love, to responsible seekers. And that I do my very, very best.

An amazing woman named Gayle Highpine has written a profound article about culture appropriation regarding white people drinking Ayahuasca. In it, she shares an essential bit of wisdom that I have also been continuously struck by in my time in the Amazon. She writes:

> *Amazonian indigenous people are not concerned about the ethnicity of practitioners. Amazonian indigenous people are concerned about the degradation and devaluation of their*

profession by practitioners they consider imposters, regardless of skin color.[19]

To her first point, I have personally spent months and months of my life in the Amazon and Andes, studying the ethical and traditional methods of working with Ayahuasca and Huachuma. During no occasion did I ever receive anything but love and acceptance by the tribes that carry this wisdom. That includes the members of the tribes who don't identify as medicine people; they still hold reverence for anyone preserving the sacredness of these practices. It was, in fact, my first indigenous teacher who looked me in the eyes and called me a shaman. I have been moved to sobbing tears by his and others' generosity and acceptance. I sincerely have never felt judged. And believe me; my sensitive, self-loathing nature was sniffing it out for years. It never came. That spoke volumes.

That said, what Ms. Highpine states about the concern they carry for imposters is very, very real as well. It's a concern that burns deep in me too. It is an incredible insult to assume you know what it takes to honor this unbelievably holy and difficult path just because you've had a handful of ceremonies and you feel the call. That isn't enough to justify taking the plunge and leading a ceremony. It IS enough to justify a sincere interest and an invitation to do the work to become a legitimate practitioner.

I wonder, too, why we aren't equally appalled by doctors and scientists that exhibit the elitist assumption they have the right to work with these medicines? What happened to the art of asking for permission? The disease of privilege is so incredibly pervasive in the Western world that

---

[19] *Is it Cultural Appropriation for White People to Drink Ayahuasca?* (2018) Gayle Highpine, https://kahpi.net/cultural-appropriation-ayahuasca

we have forgotten how to humbly ask for mutual consent when we interact with the universe. These plants are sentient beings, so pausing to reflect on whether or not they want to work with us, too, is literally the first step to forming a relationship of trust. Just because you have a PhD doesn't mean a plant spirit wants to dance with you.

In the Shipibo-Conibo tradition that I studied, tradition states that the apprentice shall not pour a single cup of medicine in *at least* the first seven years. Typically it takes twelve. I met one amazing shaman that apprenticed for *twenty-five years* before he poured for anyone. I BOW to his integrity. *(It took me ten years, for the record. I drank hundreds and hundreds of times—both in ceremony and alone, under the guidance of my teacher—before I was even close to owning that responsibility.)*

I will go into detail as to why this is so integral later on, but all I wish to emphasize here is this: The people entrusted to protect and honor these traditions are willingly sharing the ancient knowledge with sincere, responsible people of all skin colors. If the calling is there and the integrity to be of service is felt, they are truly color blind. But we are expected to do the glorious and difficult work.

Whoever we are.

That work never ends.

Not only have I been the recipient of many comments from Haterville (Ignorant Gringa! Know-it-all white trash! etc.), I'm also seeing an astounding number of racist comments in the medicine community at large. It does make perfect sense, as that aspect of our shadow is loud and proud in the Western world at the moment—which is wonderful as we are given the opportunity to feel it and heal it. This is just a small contribution on my part to keep the dialogue going, as that is an essential element of integration and healing.

None of us can undo the color of our skin. That's why it's such a painful thing to feel judged for; it's based in pure innocence. We are who we are. I do hold tremendous responsibility as a medicine carrier and a human being to remain honest, authentic, and continue to do this work with pure intentions. But I will not be coerced into feeling guilty, shamed, or someone *less than* because I wasn't born in another part of the world. Mamahuasca wouldn't let me.

Still, white privilege is a very real condition; it's a shadowy aspect in many of us that have been consistently given opportunities that others have to work ten times as hard for based upon the existing prejudice and systems that uplift some and suppress others. It's hard for many of us to truly grasp the reality of this condition because it's literally the antithesis of our experiences—myself included, though I may have a bit more empathy with minorities due to the fact that I'm a woman. But I still don't really know what it's like to be anything else but white in America; yet I know enough to be extremely sensitive to the fact that I have indeed benefited.

When spiritually bypassing white people show up in yoga studios with medicine they procured on the internet after a few less-than-authentic ceremonies, they implicitly and explicitly proclaim authority to hold sacred space for innocent trusting souls, and horrific repercussions often result. That is straight up arrogance and entitlement.

But in the end, this isn't so much an issue of race as it is an issue of respect and hard work. You don't get to bypass medical school and decide you're a doctor. You shouldn't be able to bypass indigenous training and still pour medicine.

Westerners need and deserve the medicine too, so it's only natural that some of us learn the art of being a carrier. I had one indigenous Maestro giggle at me once that, "I'm glad it's you who has to pour in that loco world and not me." Hah. It's funny because it's true.

When I was ready to really manifest my teacher, I wanted him or her to be from the Western world, but traditionally trained. I found that my amazing Shipibo shamans could not relate to my particular kind of crazy; it's a different world out here than the one they encounter in the jungle. I found there was a certain plateau to working with them simply because of their lack of ability to relate. And that's absolutely essential in the space of healing.

I found exactly what I had hoped to find; my main teacher is Western, and yet he spent almost two decades in the Amazon studying, drinking, and training. He was literally my dream come true. He deeply understood my psychosis, as a person who dealt with addiction and darkness himself. So I felt safe in that I was seen. And there was that sense of—well geez, if he can do it, so can I. That was a game changer for me. And I assume those I am blessed to pass on this information to feel the same.

I can't imagine having taken on this gargantuan task without the opportunity to sit next to a master, learning the ropes and watching the magic unfold. Oh my gosh we had some wild nights. My teacher taught me early on that everything in this path is deeply felt and learned through experience—I can literally count on one hand the number of times he actually gave me verbal instructions. It was always a path of watching and doing, and refining my behaviors based on results.

In many ways, I learned what to do by first repeating what not to do. My teacher would rarely say anything about how I was working in ceremony; he wanted me to read the energies of his responses, of the space, of the people who sat with us, and of my own internal guidance system. I had to decipher what to do myself, but always under the safety of his watch. He wouldn't let me help the UFC fighter healing his rage until I was well equipped to do so. He wouldn't let me clear the darkness of a professional poker player until I knew how to keep myself safe from the shadow of lies. He wouldn't let me hold space for the release of sexual trauma until my own painful journey had been alchemized and soothed.

Then there was the time I learned how to do an exorcism purely from the space of love, and if I had an ounce of judgment, fear, or anger, it would give fuel to the darkness I was working with. We came face to face with demonic, terrifying forces. And after every ceremony, we found the place of lightness and laughter. It was how we let it go—wide-eyed, giggly, and grateful that all was safe and calm once more. I felt like we went into spiritual battlefields every night, and when I was his right-hand woman, I would have taken a bullet for him. In many ways, I did.

Because I know to the core of my being what it takes to do this work, I figuratively and literally bow to everyone who walks beside me, who came before me, and who will continue long after me to carry on these traditions. It's going to take a massive tribe of us to continue to lift the vibration of the planet—we are all her children in the end, and she needs us in a big way right now. We need us right now; this is make-or-break-time.

My prayer is this: That we can all learn to be more supportive of each other's differences in this work, and bring less judgment, less containment, less sameness, and instead honor the wishes of the plants. It takes all kinds to create a shift in consciousness. That's why all kinds of us are called.

In the end, it's integrity that matters. Not skin color. Gender. Financial status. Age. Just our willingness to do the work, to be as honest as we can about our shadows, and to make a daily commitment to be of service in the highest way possible. In other words, let's just do our best to come from love.

Mystery #4: There Is No Such Thing as a Healer

What Does It Mean to Heal?

In the Western culture, we have come to sycophantically adore whoever we view as a "healer." Figures like John of God are literally godly to many, viewed as larger-than-life deities that possess powers we assume we could never understand.

We pay scads of money for a perceived panacea. We go head first into unusual modalities with the hopes that something will help. None of us wants to suffer.

The good news that is everything is medicine. The bad news is everything is also toxic and poisonous.

Yes, everything.

We, as individuals, determine how something interacts with us. Normally, that relationship is deeply subconscious, and not at all intuitive. But it starts and ends with personal integrity. That's why knowing ourselves is quite literally the solution to everything that ails us. The mystery of this mystery school is the mystery of self-knowledge.

When we encounter spaces of pain, we seek out fellow humans for assistance, and that's beautiful. It takes a tribe to help us awaken, and when we use each other as spiritual mirrors and support systems to go deeper within, magic awaits.

But when we turn to someone or something as a healer, hoping they can do the work for us, at the very least we are disappointed, and at the worst, our suffering increases tenfold. Even if we think it works. If we haven't learned the full reason for the illness or blockage, it will come back in one way or another. Lessons never, ever go unlearned. Never!

Does this mean we should ignore anyone who dubs themselves a healer and do everything on our own? Goodness no. What it does mean is it's very wise to understand the process, so we can keep our personal responsibility to achieve maximum results.

So let's figure out how healing works, and go soul-first into the magical abyss.

Western medicine is an allopathic process. The etymology of the word "allopathic" is simple: It's Greek root means "to attack the suffering." Ironically, this word was coined by Samuel Hahnemann, the godfather of homeopathic medicine.[20] Homeopathy medicine introduces minute essences of elements that incite the body to kick into its own healing process. Hahnemann used the term "allopathic" in a derogatory way to describe "heroic medicine," which was the prevailing Western viewpoint at the time.[21] From a holistic viewpoint, attacking the disease is completely counterintuitive. The body is expressing illness from a deep space of wisdom; just attacking it doesn't create healing, because with this method we never bother to uncover what it manifested in the first place.

Visit a Western medical expert and they will find a way to fight the disease that ails you. Whether through pharmaceutical means, surgery, or some other invasive system, the goal of Western medicine is to eradicate the disease, not to understand it.

But you know what happens when suffering gets attacked? More suffering is guaranteed. Attacking = conflict = resistance = suffering.

And yet, we know so little about diseases. Why do some people get them and others don't? Why does the coronavirus, as an example, not infect everyone, and equally so? Where do these diseases come from, really? Why can't we solve riddles like cancer and heart disease and Alzheimer's?

---

[20] https://www.hevert.com/market-us/en_US/company_profile/hevert_News/article/samuel-hahnemann-the-father-of-homeopathy. Last accessed May 7, 2021.
[21] https://en.wikipedia.org/wiki/Allopathic_medicine. Last accessed May 7, 2021.

Because they aren't riddles. They are information reserved solely for the vessel that contracts them. And no two illnesses—even those with the same label and diagnosis—appear and act the same. We are unique, all of us, and the way our bodies each communicate are equally personal.

Yesterday's big medical breakthrough is today's fallacy. This is because we focus on attacking—eradicating—and not understanding. We want to classify, to predict, and to compartmentalize; but sameness is not a symptom of our individuality. Healing is always, always a holistic process. And that process always involves care.

Disease is not a monster to go to war with. It's information. It's a sacred reflection of deep wisdom.

Attacking a disease is like hacking off a snake on Medusa's head. Another one always grows back.

Say you beat breast cancer with chemo and drugs. If that illness doesn't return, another will, if you haven't yet felt the reason it manifested to begin with. Maybe depression will enter in. Maybe it will show up as migraines or rage or an existential crisis. But it will return, either in this lifetime or the next. Not because it's evil or even that it wants to harm us, but because it has divine lessons in the form of emotions for us to learn, integrate, and expand with. These are sacred lessons that cannot be shrugged off.

This is why someone who turns to Ayahuasca, or any other plant medicine or healer, as a cure, does not achieve what they hoped for. You might be asking, then, why the internet is full of stories of miraculous healings and instant shifts and changes. Know that one of two things has occurred with every account of healing that you read: The individual may have not only experienced an eradication of the disease, but also integrated the deep wisdom of why this had occurred in the first place. That is really what we're aiming for; it's self-understanding that is the miracle, not a mysterious dismissal of the ailment. The other, more common scenario is that a temporary appearance of healing has manifested, fooling the person into believing the journey with that issue is complete. People don't typically return to tell the next chapter of the story, which is the return of the illness. Even more common, they don't even realize the issue has returned. Maybe they went to heal alcoholism, which never actually relapsed, but later on they developed cancer. The wisdom of what the soul wishes to learn could be encapsulated in both experiences, but if they don't know to connect the two illnesses, it appears as though one thing was cured, and now there's a new challenge to conquer.

All of life is about learning and expanding—not being free of suffering. This is the never-ending work of healing.

The Real Way We Heal Ourselves

The opposite perspective of the allopathic viewpoint is the homeopathic philosophy mentioned above. This word breaks down to mean, essentially, "similar to the suffering." It holds that like understands like. The spiritual practice of this resolves to one concrete concept. It has nothing to do with attacking, and everything to do with feeling. If allopathy, with its focus on the "allo" or *other,* looks to external causes for our suffering, homeopathy demands that we turn our attention within. And feeling is the pathway to within.

Interestingly enough, the Greek root "patheia"—found in both "allopathic" and "homeopathic"—has a triple meaning. It stands for suffering, disease, and feeling. I love that disease and feeling are synonyms here. It tells us everything we need to know. Physical disease manifests because of trapped emotions.

Feeling is healing. It's that simple. And that complex. Healing is profoundly direct, and yet profoundly difficult. These experiences are the core and fundamental reasons we exist at all. To heal is to expand, and the meaning of life is growth. So this is precisely what we are all here to experience.

Emotions are energy in motion. When we stop feeling, those emotions and energies get trapped inside us. If they're trapped long enough, they can transform into a solid form. It's pretty damn magical.

People talk about Ayahuasca and various other sacred plants all the time as healers, and in many ways, that's very accurate. Aya herself is a ridiculously potent brew that has been shown to transform all kinds of physical ailments. People with cancer have walked away healed— symptom and cancer-free. People with diabetes have had their blood sugar levels balanced. She can eradicate just about any bacteria or toxicity. Some studies have even shown she can regenerate nerves and brain cells.[22] That's miraculous!

Here's the rub: Once again, if we receive the gift of physical healing from anyone or anything, we have to understand why it manifested to begin with. No one takes away our disease, they give us a chance to see why it originally formed, and then, if we're lucky, we get to traverse through the emotions that were trapped so we are freed from ever recreating that illness—in any form.

If that process is incomplete, then so is the healing.

---

[22] *Hallucinogenic Amazonian Medicine Stimulates Generation of New Brain Cells* (2016) Benjamin Taub,
https://www.iflscience.com/brain/hallucinogenic-amazonian-medicine-stimulates-generation-of-new-brain-cells

And that's OK. This is part of the core of expansion we humans came here to learn. Since death is not a permanent destination, we have all the time in the world to figure this out. Mama Aya and her powerful plant partners are infinitely patient too. They just want us to wake up to the fact that we are the ones with the power. We are the ones that create the disease, so we are the ones that can release it as well. The kingdom of healing is within you. And we are the ultimate medicines.

To illustrate how this works, let me share a personal story.

When I first started drinking Ayahuasca, I had regular bouts with horrific migraine headaches. They were so intense I would crawl my way to a patch of darkness and hide out with muffled sobs for hours, sometimes dry heaving, sometimes spinning out in a panic attack.

In my second ceremony, Ayahuasca thrust me into a video game (appropriate, as I produced them at the time). The digital atmosphere turned aggressive and terrifying. There were rapes and murders happening throughout the environment. All kinds of atrocities played out before my eyes.

Why are you doing this? I asked her.

Get angry, she told me. Get angry at the suffering and horrors of this world.

She didn't relent until I started simmering. A simmer became a boil as she showed me specific examples from my life that enraged me.

I had never let myself feel that rage before. I would have told you then that I was not an angry person; denial is a force, and I was completely hypnotized by the idea of who I wanted to be then, not my reality. I had tried my best to be the "nice girl" full of smiles and sweetness. Anger didn't fit into my identity. It wasn't OK or safe to feel this rage. Angry women were hysterical, typecast, ignored, and even abhorred. I didn't want to be That Girl.

As I started to let myself feel my genuine anger, all the energy rushed up to the center of my head. BOOM. Migraine time. I started sobbing. These emotions terrified and paralyzed me. This is exactly why I didn't want to feel this rage. The migraine pulsed and throbbed and I purged and wretched.

I felt rage at the things that had happened to me; events I attempted to mentally sugar coat and spiritually bypass. You know the drill... adopting the old, "It's all good" philosophy before that's actually genuine. See, in my spiritual journey, I adeptly adopted the higher perspective that everything happens for a reason and there's no such thing as a victim. These are beautiful viewpoints, but they denied the truth of how I was feeling.

I felt anger at the men who had personified and used me. I seethed at the women who lied to me and engaged in painful competition. In my past, there were two female best friends, at different phases of my life, who abruptly dropped me like a maggot-infested mango. I stored that heartbreak inside my body, held it in unexplored corners, and then lied to myself that I had recovered from the betrayal. Why? Because that felt easier than feeling the truth of how much I hurt. And because in my mind, that was the spiritual thing to do.

It turns out the spiritual thing to do is just be freaking honest already and feel what was always there.

So we traversed my personal history, turning over stones and discovering rage. Memories flashed at light speed and I purged and wretched and sobbed. Then MamaAya got to the heart of it all: my anger at God, source, the universe. I saw images of animals suffering in fires.

Images of children beaten and abused. Images of the earth ravaged and trampled and betrayed. It was as if the entire vast ocean of suffering overcame me, and I raged at the injustice of it all. Why in the hell is there so much suffering? What kind of God creates such heinous experiences for innocent beings?

Bullseye, Mama whispered. You don't trust life, sweet girl. You have to feel this to know the truth. You can't think your way to enlightenment.

The shaman came over and sang to me then, his hands on my head, pulling out the darkness. He pivoted to my temple and sucked out a huge nugget of black tar.

We both purged.

He patted me on the head and told me, "Esta bien, Gatita." It's OK, kitty cat.

When he walked away, I knew without a doubt that my migraines were in the bucket. And Aya was quick to tell me why. She said that because I was willing to feel my anger, she and the shaman were able to help me release the energy.

I rejoiced at this understanding, but she didn't let me off the hook. The rest of the night still reigns as one of top three most challenging experiences I've had with her. This is because the trip into rage had to be complete. Sometimes I fought it, and that was nightmarish. The only way out was feeling.

She also shared with me this simple truth: You are healed—for now. Stop feeling your emotions again, girl, and you will get sick again— maybe with headaches, maybe with something different. That's OK, she said, you know the secret to healing.

Fast forward 12 years. I started experiencing intense stomach pains, right in the center of my solar plexus. They lasted for almost a year before I received the diagnosis of gallstones and a septic gallbladder. In studying the Eastern wisdom about these suckers, one thing comes up a lot: The gallbladder holds anger, as it partners with the liver. More specifically, it holds resentment. This was familiar territory.

So I worked with the new manifestations of my anger. The resentment I was carrying traced back to the way my teacher and I separated. I loved that man more than I have ever loved another human; he was my hero, my sanctuary, my tether to the medicine world. I had dreams of taking bullets for his family, of going into battle with him, of giving up anything and everything to do this work side by side. Yes, I had seen aspects of his shadow, and knew that he carried the pain of abandonment, as many before me had left him. They had their reasons. I would never, ever be that girl, though.

Until I was. Until I realized the pedestal I had given him was never warranted, and the inevitable occurred. We had a mutual fall from grace with each other that still ranks as the hardest chapter of my life. The relationship absolutely exploded, and my entire journey with the medicine dissolved along with that sacred bond.

I had been left alone, without my teacher and guide, without access to the medicine I loved more than life. And I had attempted to mentally process this colossal loss, rather than feel the black abyss of emotions this had triggered.

I turned to various healers and modalities to work with these emotions, and I'm on the other side now. When I think of my teacher and the events that occurred, I can sincerely smile now, with gratitude and love. I am no longer pretending that I accept and appreciate every event that unfolded; I mean it with my whole heart. The resentment and betrayal are releasing; it's taken a few years, but hey, it takes what it takes. My gallbladder, however, has never been happier.

What a Healer Really Does

Yes, the shaman and all other legitimate healers play integral roles in this process, just like mine did in the story above. I am completely, utterly reverent about what that magical medicine man helped me do; that's a core reason I dedicated myself to this path too. Just because we are wholly responsible for our condition does not mean we can't help each other kickstart or deepen the healing process. To the contrary, a healer can be simply someone who somehow helps remind us that we can only heal oneself, or remind us that healing is even an option.

What a healer does not do is eradicate our illness for us. Those that do try to take our pain must first grapple with that energy themselves, as it does not disappear. The shaman who helped me was only able to do so because I was getting down into the root of why my illness had manifested to begin with. I was acting with complete accountability. He saw what was happening and came in to assist. It was the perfect storm, but only possible because I made it so.

Most importantly, if we don't integrate the lessons of the sickness, eventually it will manifest again; into gallstones or blindness or cancer, or whatever it is our souls suspect we will actually pay attention to.

A true healer is a vessel, which is no small task, mind you.[23] A true healer works first and foremost their whole lives to be a clear, purified

---

[23] It may seem that this sort of "vessel" is peculiar to the shamanic or nonwestern traditions, but Plato's The Ion treats the capacity to chant poetry in a similar fashion—the performer acts not through their own art, but through opening to divine inspiration. "For not by art or knowledge about

being. The less toxic and the more conscious they are, the more powerful they can be as a channel for divine energy. A true healer is always, always working on their own well-being, too. A true healer inspires us to do that same kind of work. He or she awakens us to know that healing is even possible; many of us live out our lives assuming pain and suffering just is. These are the people that can motivate us to find our own path of evolution, joy, and aliveness.

So if you visit a healer who knows that we heal ourselves in partnership with divinity, then you're in immaculate hands. They can hold space and call in that energy, allowing us to have a different perspective of ourselves and our disease. And miraculous things can happen. In an instant, we can feel and understand why we were sick to begin with. And in an instant, that energy can move and set us free.

No one can do it for us. They can only help empower us to unravel the mystery of how to do it ourselves. But it IS possible.

It's also imperative to stress that illness is not an enemy to eradicate, it's a divine message to be wholly welcomed and appreciated. We aren't meant to be trapped in a body for all of eternity, so some of them manifest both as messages and as a portal to let us go home.

Thank, er, God for that. I don't know about you, but 80-100 years at a time in duality is plenty for me.

I have seen several beautiful souls come to the medicine for healing, and what they received wasn't a physical release, but a spiritual one. One woman in particular came not even knowing she was sick. Aya kept

---

Homer do you say what you say, but by divine inspiration and by possession...You ask, 'Why is this?' The answer is that you praise Homer not by art but by divine inspiration." The singer does not sing, but is sung. See Plato, *Ion*, verse 535b, Lane Cooper translation.

preparing her for what she called "the boom." During our third ceremony, she got up to use the bathroom and nearly knocked me flat with her wing. When I told her what happened the next morning, I expected her to giggle with surprise. Instead, she fully owned her recklessness—she was aware her wings were out and admitted to showboating a bit. This absolutely delighted us both. Then she had an experience of complete surrender in her final ceremony, and left telling us she knew she was eternal.

Six weeks later, she was diagnosed with leukemia, and she died shortly thereafter. She left us with full grace and surrender. She was not afraid. What healed in her was the resistance to death, not the disease that was there to usher her back into the cosmos.

Disease is not the enemy. Nor is it "allo," the *other*. Nothing is. It's all just information. We can go to a healer from any tradition and receive a reflection of what might be going on. Then it's up to us to figure out what our bodies are telling us, and to invite in the emotions so the energy can move. We must somehow respond to that information, and do so with everything we've got, and then everything we haven't.

This is why our medical system is broken, at its core. We trust our doctors to tell us everything we need to know about how to fight the sickness too. It doesn't work that way. Only we can know why something has manifested because only we can access our feelings and the truth of our path so far. We can rely on healers to offer wisdom, sacred space, powerful tools, and partnership—but nothing more. In order to care for and even heal ourselves, we must focus our attention on what the illness is teaching us. That means opening to the truth.

If you're sick and you would prefer not to be, in addition to whatever treatment you feel called to use, start telling yourself the truth of how you feel. Be honest about how you've felt your whole life. Revisit the spaces and memories that feel stuck and painful. Be a detective to your internal process and see if you can find the roots. Or reach to Ayahuasca for help in the illumination. Or a great psychotherapist. Or a spiritual coach who knows how to hold space and to illuminate the shadow.

You know you're making progress when two things happen: 1) You hit a spot inside of you that rages with resistance, fear, or pain. You find a core wound that you may have never even known consciously; you hit the jackpot of emotions. 2) You also start feeling releases; things open up inside in a spacious, expansive way, and you see and feel those changes in your body and in your life. Healing is not just about feeling the emotions, but making the changes in our lives that support this new healthier perspective. Relationships often change. Priorities most certainly do. It's a game of self-discovery, coupled with the courage to stay honest about what we are feeling. Whatever you do, remain responsible. Stay open to hearing and feeling the truth of your situation. Know that you are not being punished or tortured, despite what it may seem. And that no matter what, it will be OK. "Esta bien, Gatita." It's OK, kitty cat.

We suffer so damn much in these bodies and minds sometimes. But this is why we get to exit. We deserve to rest. Illness is often the angel that takes us there, despite being labeled an evil "other" that we ought to learn to kill. But the truth is, disease loves us enough to play the villain and takes us back into the arms of unconditional love. As Ram Dass beautifully sang it, "We are all walking each other home." The same is true for every emotion, every teardrop, every moment of suffering. It's all designed to awaken and expand us. It's all designed to remind us of how powerful, sacred, and immortal each one of us really is.

All Things Are Possible

As a point of inspiration, I would like to share a list of miracles I have either experienced myself, or have been blessed to witness. Please note that all of these moments of spontaneous healing came from intensely hard work, accountability, integrity, and the willingness to keep showing up for ourselves in our continued healing. This is not a light-switch experience, but the process of owning our responsibility to heal ourselves, in every moment.

Disease isn't permanent—nothing is. Which means healing isn't permanent either. We are always on the journey of learning and expanding in these lifetimes; that necessitates we pay attention, and do our best to enjoy the ride.

Yet we must know what is possible so we have the courage to dream.

Spoiler alert: Anything is.

An incomplete list of magical moments I have witnessed and/or experienced within the container of sacred ceremony:

- A woman diagnosed with type 2 diabetes did one single ceremony, had a massive breakdown of crying fits and purging, and has had stable blood sugar ever since.

- A man seeking healing from the loss of his brother discovers his daughter holds the soul of his deceased twin. He leaves absolutely certain his little girl is the reincarnation of his beloved sibling.

- My personal exorcism, where horrendously dark energies are taken from me after 1.5 hours of doctoring, releasing me from the throes of relapsed bulimia and alcoholism. This initiated profound lessons about protection, discernment, and accountability.

- A woman with kidney disease does a four-night cycle, then heads to her doctor the next week, only to find her kidneys look ten years younger. She is alive and healthy still today.

- A man who killed someone in his youth for raping his younger sister finds peace and forgiveness for both the deceased and himself.

- A man living as a raging alcoholic, about to lose his wife and his family, shows up for three consecutive cycles; he is now thriving as a top executive, has repaired his entire family dynamic, and has been sober for over a year.

- A woman who hasn't spoken to her father in 20 years receives the message that her dad has just 1.5 years to live and that it's imperative she heals that relationship before he transitions. She does so in earnest; 1.5 years later, he dies while she is in ceremony. She is endlessly grateful she had a chance to repair her bond with her one and only daddy.

- I spent an evening searching the cosmos for my deceased soul kitty, Mr. Boo, and couldn't find him anywhere. My entire relationship with the afterlife and faith in our immortal souls fell apart, and just as I was succumbing to the wildly intense grief, Mr. Boo emerged from my heart and laid on my lap. I giggled at the notion that I ever thought he'd leave me; faith that all things come from and return to love restored.

- A woman whose son suffered from schizophrenia due to head trauma in a car crash asked to use her body as a vessel to heal her son. After multiple ceremonies, he became well enough to live on his own; a miracle as his independence was never projected to be possible again.

- A woman in her sixties who had never known joy came to ceremony as a last resort, suicidal and despondent. After three ceremonies, her life force returned; she felt genuinely happy for the first time in her adult life. She is still doing the work to cultivate her claim to the light, and gets better every month.

There are so. Many. More. Truth be told, every single ceremony brings magic and miracles I will never be aware of for the people that reenter the world and experience their new states of consciousness. But if you dream it—and WORK for it—it is possible with these plants.

Mystery #5: Psychonauts Beware: Key Elements to Safe Journeys

Anything that has the power to heal the deepest wounds and traumas can also cause them as well. It is therefore imperative that we prepare our bodies, minds, and beings with great care and effort before we go spelunking into the unknown.

You Shall Not Pass: Warnings About Preexisting Conditions and Medications

Plant medicines do not mix well with many pharmaceutical drugs; especially SSRIs, MAOIs, opiates, and heart medications.

In addition to mindfulness around drug complications, there are some illnesses and diagnoses that also require extreme caution or abstinence in the name of safety too. This is not a complete list, so if you have health or mental challenges, consult a plant medicine expert such as a Shamanic Practitioner or Psychedelics Integration Coach, or even your family doctor, before you embark on any plant medicine journey to make sure you are safe. And always, always make sure your practitioner knows everything about your health history and prescriptions before you proceed.

Here are some preexisting conditions that raise major red flags in the entheogen space:

- Heart Conditions: If you've had a history of heart issues like palpitations, damaged valves, heart attacks, heart disease, or extremely high blood pressure, medicines like Ayahuasca and Iboga can be deadly. Most medicines increase blood pressure due to the intensity, so protect your heart.

- Cancer: Most practitioners welcome individuals with this diagnosis, as long as they aren't in the process of active chemotherapy. Both the toxicity of chemo and the related medications can have serious side effects with psychotropics.

- Epilepsy: If you have a history of medical seizures (as opposed to those caused by injuries), plant medicines can be dicey. Since substances like Ayahuasca can induce a seizure, and as a result make you susceptible to purging and choking, you must be supervised at all times by someone experienced with this issue.

- Pregnancy: Some medicines are gentle enough for expectant mothers and their babies, but many are not. Even non-psychotropic plants like Sage, a ubiquitous tool in many ceremony spaces, can cause spontaneous miscarriages, so this requires full awareness by the practitioner and gentle dosages if you are called at all. The same is true for mothers who are breastfeeding.

- Schizophrenia: For those dealing with a confusing relationship with reality, plant medicines can worsen this state of confusion and lack of grounding. I do not recommend anyone with this diagnosis to experiment with altered spaces.

- Bipolar or Manic Depression: This one is tricky because medicines like Ayahuasca can work wonders to help balance the neurotransmitters in our brains; however, many experts still purport that the risks are too dangerous to proceed. Let your practitioner know if you work with these issues, and they can potentially chart a course of microdosing and coaching that can help safely prepare you for a deeper dive. This is not possible, however, if you are taking any medications like SSRIs or MAOIs. These can cause a condition called Serotonin Syndrome, when combined with plant medicines, which has a dangerous or even deadly effect.

The big message here is this: Communicate every known issue and concern to the people you are trusting with your physical, mental, and emotional safety; leave nothing to chance. While plant medicines are divinely healing, they can worsen some conditions, and require the utmost respect before imbibing. Thanks to increases in decriminalization and legalization, we are seeing more and more fantastic research and scientific studies revealing the truth of how they work with our bodies, but we are years and years away from definitive information about each plant and each condition. Please be safe and cautious.

How to Prepare for an Entheogenic Journey

There are a few key elements to follow before any deeply altered trip through the cosmos; preparing the body, mind, and spirit is essential to having an enjoyable and rewarding ride.

Body Preparations

Most medicines require at least a few days of clean eating free of things like garlic, spices, salt, sugar, heavy oils, animal fats and proteins, dairy, and fermented foods. What can you eat? Feast on organic fruits and veggies (low salt and sugar varieties), eggs, plain chicken, freshwater fish, and whole grains. The cleaner your diet is, the less likely you will have to feel discomfort due to yesterday's burger. That's a big, big bonus.

In addition to preparing the body for a dance with the medicines, the simple and bland diet also brings in the magic of giving something in order to receive in return. Many of us are rather unstructured in daily lives, so taking on the task to be restricted and intentional in how we treat our bodies is a beautiful way to help the mind realize the benefit of discipline too. And it also expresses to the spirit of the medicines that we are ready and willing to work for the things we are seeking. We get what we give after all.

Mind Preparations

The single most impactful practice to undertake before a journey is a devotion to meditation. Whether you practice the art of presence through traditional seated silence, dance, guided meditations, sound therapy, bodywork, or literally any other method that helps you anchor your consciousness somewhere other than the mind, it's precious practice for surrendering into the plant medicine abyss.

Sitting with sacred plants is a meditation all its own, but Ayahuasca in particular tells me frequently that "we shouldn't do our homework on the teacher's desk." This means the more we prepare for a graceful journey, the more the medicines themselves tend to reward us in return. There are no shortcuts to awakening, and it really does happen one breath at a time.

Most medicines also require abstinence from sexual activity at least three days before diving in. This is because the expression of sexual union is a huge movement of energy, and we need all the life force we can muster for a monster trip with plant medicine. Additionally, the intimate act of sexual union can bring on all kinds of complexities— emotions, energies, entanglements, etc. The plants prefer that we come as clean, purified, and grounded as possible; last night's one-night stand does not set us up for success in this regard. Some even say the plants themselves are jealous. All I know is that Ayahuasca wants my full attention when I go to her, so purifying—for at least a few days—is a key component to having a loving and connected time with her.

It's also imperative that you feel certain you have the stability to handle an experience that may literally turn your life—and the perspectives you hold on reality—upside down. We all would like to think we're prepared for a massive shift in consciousness, but when it happens, we often receive the news with horror and resistance. Change is tough for a mind to embrace, and a complete restructuring of how we see the world is no easy task. If you have any uncertainty in this department, consult a psychedelic therapist or coach, or talk to your plant medicine facilitator. They will be able to help you determine if and when it's safe to journey.

Emotional Preparations

Here's a word to the wise: Stay away from the news, horror flicks, and any dark media a week or so before you journey; it's just abhorrent to process a violent news clip rather than the juicy parts of our own personal lives. We want to do deep shadow work and cosmic exploration, not replay a frightening special effect.

Additionally, anything you do to create a feeling of safety for the vulnerable part of you to feel and process your emotions is a priceless exercise before an entheogenic trip. Since the core of healing lies in having the capacity to deeply feel, things like inner child world, somatic therapy, and a core commitment to giving yourself permission to feel ANYTHING is positively golden. Consent to being loved deeply.

Managing Expectations

This last piece is the trickiest one. Many of us go to plant medicines for deeply desired healing, and it's true that some of us see these beings as our last resort.

Here's the truth of what lies before you:

Miracles are possible, even probable, and it will be an unforgettable experience unlike anything you've lived through so far. Your wildest dreams and wishes may be absolutely honored and even surpassed, as the potency of these spaces to rewire our minds and release our demons is bona fide and magical. However, the more we cling to or attach to specific results, the more they often evade us. Plant medicines heal us through the back door of our consciousness, and it can take a long, long time before we become aware of the shifts and changes inside of us. Some folks are on the fast track, but the truth of it is, most of us take years to heal the wounds inside our hearts; those took years to develop, too.

So enter into every blessed ceremony with a couple of core, sacred intentions. Feel them with your entire being. Let your heart call out with longing to the vulnerable requests you hold deep inside. But as soon as you take the medicine, do your best to just let it all go. Let the medicine carry you through the experience however it sees fit; I guarantee it won't be the way you expect. If that were the case, your expectant mind could have already healed you. No, these uber-wise beings must do exactly what we don't expect, in a way that literally blows our minds. That's where the healing happens.

The more we are attached to any certain outcome, the more the plants— and the universe—have to evade us, like a dangling carrot hanging in front of a starving horse's face. We do not chase down and demand our deepest desires, we crack open our hearts, create a deeply felt invitation, and let the universe work her magic. Easy to talk about, intensely difficult to execute. But our best is always good enough, as we are only here to learn.

Be Ridiculously Discerning About Who You Trust to Keep You Safe

In my work as a shamanic/psychedelic integration coach, I hear all the time from people that did their best to surrender to a powerful psychotropic plant in what they thought was a safe container, and ended up piling on more trauma instead of releasing past pains. This is the opposite of what we intend when we get courageous and alter our consciousness in a sacred ceremony. However, because the work of a shaman is not typically monitored in any way (nor should it be by the Western world), it's hard to know when we're actually in safe hands.

Aside from the plant or brew itself, the individual facilitating any plant or psychedelic journey is literally the most important piece of the complicated puzzle. Why? Because they are the vessel by which the consciousness of the plant will come through. They are the one responsible for creating a safe container, and if that doesn't occur, participants are likely to feel it and very likely end up worse off. The shaman is the conductor; their vibration will be felt by all, and it's the foundation for what the plant works with as it enters the space. If that frequency is disruptive, unsettled, or inexperienced, this will show up in the space. The more sensitive the participant is, the more they will feel this dissonance.

As a facilitator of hundreds and hundreds of plant ceremonies, I can attest to how what I'm working with on the inside unmistakably shows up in the space I'm working in. And if I'm doing my own shadow exploration outside of the ceremonies I hold, the people that trust me with their spiritual lives will feel it.

Of course, the reverse is true too. It's an awesome, intensely important responsibility.

This work takes a ridiculous amount of commitment, training, understanding, and humility. And no matter how good your intentions are, if you haven't done the work—and continue that honest self-discovery until the day you die—the people who trust you are at risk.

And please, whatever you do, make sure you sit with people who have traditional training. Don't let the Western world fool you into trusting a certification; only a true apprenticeship allows a shaman to be born.

Yes, it's true that no two shamanic facilitators do this work exactly the same. So why on earth is it so essential that we receive traditional training?

There's a gazillion reasons. I'll cover a few.

By far the most important factor in why it's essential to source an experienced teacher to learn from lies in the power of the ego. The operating system we all carry that creates the perception of control and knowingness is a tricky beast indeed.

Since our minds/egos are not the part of our consciousness we access for spiritual work, it's essential that we repeatedly learn how to connect with wisdom that is much deeper than the thoughts in our head. Yet the fundamental question we all ask is—how? How do we know the communication we're receiving is not from our own minds?

The real answer is—we don't. Even 15 years into this incredible training, I struggle with this at times and have to seek honest feedback from peers, elders, and the medicine herself.

In the shamanic integration coaching I do, the people that come to me with the most traumatic experiences from ceremonies often have one thing in common: They sat with a self-trained facilitator, or one that didn't complete the years and years necessary to be trusted. These folks, however well meaning, have not had the benefit of getting direct and honest feedback from someone further on the path than they are. Additionally, I have found that anyone brazen enough to think it's possible to teach yourself the mysteries of medicine work quite often have a very grandiose ego, and that's a dangerous energy to trust in ceremony.

Think of it this way: Would you trust a self-taught surgeon? Chiropractor? Veterinarian?

When we humbly give ourselves over to learn the lineage of a being we respect and wish to emulate in shamanic spaces, we allow ourselves to first learn the tradition of shamanic work. There is a point in every apprentice's journey where it becomes time to stand on their own, and that's a very personal decision emerging from refined self-awareness. That typically takes no less than seven years—sometimes volumes more. But without a core foundation of traditional and passed-down wisdom, we are walking on very shaky ground. This walk is almost always also an ordeal.

Stepping forth as a leader of intensely profound and vulnerable plant medicine ceremonies precipitates a deep level of trust in oneself. Yet the most important trait any shamanic guide can carry is this: Humility.

How do we both have the chutzpah to proclaim ourselves capable of protecting souls AND be a sincerely humble being? That right there takes a tremendous amount of self-discovery and shadow work. The reluctant shaman is the safe one. The one who rushes the process and is arrogant enough to assume they can bypass the protocol that's existed for thousands of years—he/she is dangerous.

I have never met a facilitator that lacks traditional training that is not coming from ego. This is tricky, as many of these folks truly are well intended. Many also have a sincere connection to the medicine. None of that matters if the energies of a ceremony blast through the cosmos and send participants into a frenzy, only to find they are left with an inexperienced and bamboozled guide who is faking their way through the process.

When we are deep inside Ayahuasca's embrace, we are cracked open and oh-so-vulnerable. If the person that comes to us in assistance is terrified, inexperienced, or otherwise does not trust that everything is going to be OK, that is deeply felt. I have watched helpers go with sincerity to assist someone in a deep process but without the tools to do so, and it can go horribly wrong. I've seen them pass out, yell and scream at participants, bolt out of the ceremony space in terror, and completely freeze up and fail to assist. This is heavy work indeed.

We have to know what we know, and even more important, be humble enough to know what we don't know.

My teacher would tell me that if we are not as grounded as the earth itself, connected to our beingness and trusting the medicine to our core, we have absolutely no business helping someone else through a challenging altered space. Remember how the road to hell was paved? Right-o, good intentions.

Thousands and thousands of people are hearing the call to facilitate ceremonies these days, and that's a beautiful thing—the medicine doesn't reproduce, she recruits. And it will take an army of us to continue to transform consciousness.

Because we humans tend to lack patience and are uber fond of the turbo-route, there are multiple courses and programs showing up that promise to teach and train participants in a matter of weeks or months. These programs may contain valuable information and experiences, but no one becomes a master of anything in a matter of weeks or months. The well-meaning programs in this category are, at best, a place to get started in the path, and at worst a scam to give a false sense of mastery in exchange for a hefty fee. Regardless, folks that graduate from these programs often know little more than people who have drank 30+ times as participants.

In his book *Outliers*, Malcolm Gladwell popularized the threshold of 10,000 hours as a foundation for mastery. The idea is that this is the pinnacle of becoming an expert at something, which equates to about 417 days of intentional practice and focus. Please keep this in mind when you trust your personal safety to anyone, for any reason.

The courses I mentioned above can be valuable as a knowledge-share, but they do not—under any circumstance—have the authority to name you a shaman or facilitator. That always, always comes from the plants. And it always, always comes from YEARS of experience.

There is no shortcut to becoming a doctor, a lawyer, a psychologist, or a professor. And there is no shortcut to spending years and years understanding the nuances of energetic and spiritual communication + protection.

To those very rare, very few among us out there who just innately came into this world knowing how to hold sacred space, how to navigate the wildly erratic energies of a plant like Ayahuasca, and how to keep themselves and others safe in perilous and vulnerable altered experiences—bless you to pieces. You are a unicorn and I honor you.

As a participant, however, I personally would never trust my safety to anyone who hasn't done the work. Plant diets are a must, otherwise the mystery of plant consciousness still prevails, and safety cannot be guaranteed. A lineage is a must—otherwise there is no firm foundation to use for self-discovery. Hundreds and hundreds and hundreds of ceremonies are also pivotal—otherwise there are just too many mysterious scenarios that the facilitator won't know how to handle.

Sitting next to my teachers for 10 years helped me know that I can handle whatever Ayahuasca throws my way. But even then, my training is never really done.

Don't risk sitting with someone who seems well intended and sincere but lacks the experience to back up those warm fuzzies with results. Your spiritual and emotional well-being is far, far too precious.

A Call to All Ceremony Guides: Please Be Humble Enough to Know When You Are Not Ready

Assuming the role of shaman and healer is a sexy path indeed. The ego adores the accolades, the pedestals, the fanfare. But those inflations come crashing down the moment we are in over our heads, and at that point, there is no turning back. Please, if you are reading this and you know in your heart you haven't had the training to guide people through a dark night of the soul, take a step back, do your own work, find a teacher that will guide and validate you, and keep us all—and you—safe and protected.

This is in no way meant to discourage anyone from doing this sacred work. We need as many sincere and strong beings answering the calling as the plants can muster. But there is a path to this role, and there is no avoiding the work. You can't drink Ayahuasca 30 times and self-proclaim you are ready to pour. That requires years of apprenticing and guidance—and even then, it's never guaranteed that you'll really be ready. That's up to the plants, not us. We can only do our best.

But for all of us that feel that calling—answer it. Throw yourself into this incredible journey. Be willing to sacrifice any aspect of your lives that doesn't align. Find a teacher and a lineage that speaks to your soul. And enjoy the ride; it's the most magical, demanding, mysterious, and beautiful path imaginable. But do not try to find a way around the necessary training and work.

Testimony #3: Michael J. Patwin

Private Aviation Executive, Artist, Plant Messenger

One early morning, I sat with Rapé and finally grokked why they call it 'sitting' with him; indeed, why plants often are attributed gender. The moment mirrored watching my grandfather sit in his wooden chair, feet caked with mud, overlooking his fields in rural Tennessee from the side of his peach brick rambler. He would unveil homegrown tobacco from his jacket pocket. Pinch and fold it, offer it out for me to smell. Then tuck it into his mouth clumsily, sit and lean back, offering his wrinkled brow up to the sun.

Plants soothe us. They stimulate us. They dance with our chemistry and help us alchemize the emotion under the surface, splinters of thoughts tweezed into consciousness. The plant medicine we do is for us; yet not only for us. Likewise, 'The Work' from our sits with these powerful entities is primarily the aftermath we call integration. How we honor and apply the homework the plants gave us; how much we choose to bring those alchemized intentions into consciousness. In circle, we light the fire during the ceremony part; the flame, the smoke, and its cleansing is the integration. It could alter our lives in millimeters or miles. It's our choice.

I can't remember my grandfather's eyes or recall him looking into mine. He's always been a silhouette of a man in overalls among a field of friends.

Michael J. Patwin

Mystery #6: Plant Powers, Activate! The Master Plants as Superheroes

The Plants Are in Charge

The shamans define a master plant as one who acts as a teacher to humanity. In truth, all plants are masters in this way; even Poison Hemlock teaches us invaluable lessons about consciousness, but not exactly in a way that inspires longevity. Socrates, who lived for the truth that he knew only that he knew nothing, drank the hemlock that was poured for him. This is why shamanism has identified plants that are both full of wisdom and willing to teach us in a way that we can embody and integrate. This is the dance of death and life, light and dark.

In the Shipibo-Conibo tradition and related traditions from the Amazon, there are a few dozen core plants that are embraced as the Masters. Ayahuasca, Chacruna, Huachuma, and the psychotropic crew all belong here, of course. But so does a long list of lesser-known powerhouses, such as Chiric Sananga, Bobinsana, Coca, Ajo Sacha, and many more.

Additionally, the Northern world is teeming with teacher plants too. Some are common in our culture, like Rose, Lavender, Sage and Tobacco. Others are not as well known but equally powerful, like Tulsi, Cypress, Juniper, and Mugwort.

It's therefore unequivocally true that a plant does not have to hold the power to knock our socks off in an altered state in order to be a powerful teacher and ally. But it sure doesn't hurt.

As I write this, I'm three weeks deep in a master plant diet with Coca. Yes, the Coca in Coca-Cola. Yes, the Coca that, when chemically altered, produces Cocaine. But I guarantee you she's not at all like you'd expect her to be.

This is my eleventh plant dieta. I keep going back to this incredible process because it always helps me find my edges, and to expand past them, discovering more of what I'm made of.

These diets also create an impenetrable ally in whatever plant we convene with. Coca and I, we were already friends. Now, we are Jay-Z and Beyoncé style partners. For life. And that's magical.

Before I started on this plant path fifteen years ago, I didn't even consider that plants might have consciousness. Now, I know some plants better than I know my mother or my best friend. This is all because of the ancient and sacred path of a Master Plant Dieta.

It makes my heart exceedingly happy to see how many folks are drawn to connect with plant consciousness through plant dietas; it seems that exponentially more are called these days. Every single one of us, no matter what plant we join in partnership with, awaken to the urgency and sacredness of our relationship with this planet. And since her well-being is undeniably shaky (or rather, her tolerance of those threatening her livelihood is dwindling), this alone is a central reason for the call to dive deep with a Master Plant.

But there are many more reasons a plant diet is life changing. Come with me as we count the ways.

The Shamanic Tradition of Master Plant Dietas

The path of a Master Plant Dieta is central to lineages like Shipibo-Conibo, Quechua-Lamista, and Mestizo traditions. These are normally taken on by individuals who are on the path to either becoming a shamanic practitioner, or those who are committed to using plant consciousness as a means of expanding their own consciousness. Plus, healing. There is always, always healing.

For those of us whose jobs involve working with powerful and sacred plants like Ayahuasca or Huachuma, it's an absolute must to embark on a dieta every year or two. I personally would never, ever sit with someone who hasn't done at least a couple of diets. This is where the work is. The shadow dancing. Downloads from plants much more ancient and wiser than we are. The mergence with unity consciousness. And the (re)discovery of our edges as a being immersed in the experience of duality.

Isolated Dietas

There are two types of Master Plant Dietas: The traditional path is the isolated variety. These typically involve immersion into the jungle or wilderness, guidance by a Maestro or Maestra, and one rock solid master plant. Participants unplug from the world, consume very little food (and all of it intentionally bland), and enter into a primary relationship with the plant spirit for the duration; about 7-14 days, more if the individual needs some radical deep healings or teachings.

Most plants are consumed 2-3 times per day, and these dietas normally involve opening and closing in an Ayahuasca ceremony; perhaps even more frequent use of Aya too. It all depends on the plant and the facilitator. Some plants are very easy on the body and can be consumed regularly (like Ajo Sacha and Lavender), some are much tougher on the body and need regulation with both consumption and ceremony (like Chiric Sananga and Mapacho). Each Curandero/Curandera will have their own protocol, as we all have a different way the plants speak to us, but this is the general flow.

Social Dietas

The newer way to diet is called a Social or "Soft" Diet (Dieta Suave). This requires a longer commitment, typically 30 days or more, and involves a dual approach: Participants continue their lives as per usual with work, relationships, and related duties. Additionally, they are carving out time and commitment to the selected plant each day too. Strict protocols around diet, sexual activity, and recreational time are honored, just as in an isolated dieta. Because the dieter is handling life AND mergence with their plant, more time is needed to create the connection, and receive the gifts.

Both dietas are magical, and both are incredibly challenging journeys. I've been blessed to do several of both types of diet, and they have solid pros and cons.

Here's how I break down the differences of the dietas:

Isolated Dietas

Pros:

- These go deep almost immediately, as they are opened in ceremony and allow for complete immersion.

- They are intensely powerful, and you have the physical presence of a guide whenever you need them.

- You also typically have the opportunity to work with Ayahuasca before, during, and after the diet closes; she helps to strengthen the connection, keep you out of your ego/head space and be truly open to all the magic the master plant is bestowing.

Cons:

- The flipside is that these are truly intense experiences. Depending on the plant, they can also be very hard on the body and do require a high degree of stamina to successfully complete.

- The diet is your full-time job during the duration, and that includes any connection to the outside world. You have to be willing to give up all communications and completely focus on the diet.

- These can be expensive and require the ability to drop everything and head for the jungle, mountains, or related isolated spot in nature. And by all means, please make sure you are the hands and guidance of someone highly experienced with plant dietas.

Social Dietas

Pros:

- These allow you to handle your life, stay connected to your loved ones and work, and still have an epic journey with plant consciousness.

- They are typically less intense as the full focus is not solely on the plant, and therefore are a bit gentler on your mind, body and spirit.

- These also teach us to deeply appreciate more subtle expansions of consciousness, but not at all by sacrificing the profundity of the results we are seeking.

Cons:

- Because there are so many distractions in life, social dietas require more of a time commitment in order to deeply connect with the plant.

- It's also a lot to handle; following a strict diet of fresh, bland food is challenging as you will likely have to cook most if not all of your own meals, and allocating enough time for the connection is difficult when our lives are already so hectic.

- You will also likely not have the benefit of a guide in your physical presence. People like myself work with participants from a distance, and I make myself available as fast as I possibly can when needed, but some much prefer having assistance in the flesh.

The most essential part of any dieta is selecting the Master Plant. This happens in partnership with your shamanic guide, and it's dependent on the benefits you are seeking as a participant. There are dozens and dozens of Master Plants to choose from; some are common in our vernacular (like Rose or Sage) and some are likely to be new acquaintances (like Bobinsana or Noya Rao).

Each plant has its own personality, superhero powers, and gifts to bestow. They each work with the body and spirit in different ways, so it's essential that you are working with someone who understands the plant well; otherwise contraindications with medications, behavioral patterns, and similar health elements can occur.

It is absolutely, positively crucial to employ a guide for any dieta; isolated or social. Choosing to embark on a dieta without a protector is like going into battle without armor. It's dicey at best; these are not spaces that most of us inherently know how to handle. So if you're ready to dive in, find an experienced dieta Maestro or Maestra and follow their protocol with your whole heart. The partnership between you, the plant, and your guide is infinitely sacred and powerful.

In my journey thus far, I've dieted eleven times on nine different plants. I repeated my first diet because, like many of us, I just didn't get it right out of the gate and needed a do-over. Every single deep dive with plant consciousness is a profound learning experience. Dietas, for me, have been the game changers.

Sage taught me the very innate, impossible-to-describe space of protection and safety. She helped me to experience the most heightened place of purification and empowerment I've ever known. And she's my #1 go-to in every ceremony experience I do now; she's my proverbial American Express Card, I never, ever leave my body without her.

Lavender did wonders for my nervous system, and gave me my first tangible experience of being wholly, completely present; without resistance, and with great joy. She's the ultimate chill-out medicine, and she brings to the surface the awareness of why we resist serenity.

Ayahuasca was another dieta; yes, you can diet psychotropic plants, but obviously with extreme caution and guidance. I turned to her during a difficult time in my journey with plant medicine; I needed clarity on my path. She delivered in grand fashion by being the catalyst for a complete and total breakdown in every aspect of my world.

And then came the breakthrough.

This one was by far the most impactful, as expected. I truly felt like I wasn't ready, but it's impossible to really be ready for that kind of transformation.

Yet I wouldn't be a curandera without their divine assistance.

Ajo Sacha unlocked the secrets of the subconscious, and the collapse of typical dualistic structures. They taught me the intertwining of masculine and feminine (as such, I refer to Ajo as "they"), the language of symbols, the falsehood of time as a construct, and they also showed me, with complete clarity, my human neurosis. Which then empowered me to transcend much of that destructive behavior, one day at a time.

My master plant diet on Rose taught me what love really means, by first showing me the false ways in which I held love through imprinted constrictions and conditions. She rocked my love life and helped me to change course, and she shone her light on every way in which I was still abusing myself. She's a sweet one, Miss Rose, but the lady has some serious thorns. As the feminine always does.

Then I entered the space of Cactus Love with Huachuma. He's a life changer too. He helped me to feel and connect with my heart in a much more concrete way, and the secrets of the universe are ever more illuminated, in every moment. He oozes wisdom, but he demands integrity and the strength to own our shit, too. He's taught me patience, compassion, and the ability to just be with nature. Not do. Not think. Not obsess over whatever the mind has a focus on. Instead, to feel my heart, to flow, to trust, and to be truly present. I know now why we call him San Pedro; Saint Peter holds the keys to the gates of heaven, and so does this incredible cactus.

I turned to Juniper next for help in finally cleaning up all the old patterns of alcoholism in both myself and my lineage. I had long since kicked a full-fledged drinking problem, but still had the obsessive thoughts about drinking, and I was sick of moderating and pivoting those impulses. Because I was a big fan of gin back-in-the-day, I knew Juniper could handle this request. It worked. Magically. My relationship with alcohol is now the healthiest I could have ever imagined. And my goodness did this magnificent tree bring me oodles and glitter-coated joy.

Next up was Bobinsana; often the first dieta in the Shipibo lineage, in part because she's so damn joyful and supportive. In a euphoric sense, this was the best week of my life, communing with her. I have never felt my heart in such a profoundly deep way. She also taught me how addicted most of us are to the identification with our suffering. Her guidance is a precious reminder that transformation and growth do not have to be full of pain and difficulties. She is utterly priceless, and her medicine should be ubiquitous in our culture. Who doesn't need a stronger experience of self-love?

Last, but certainly not least, there's my current diet with Mama Coca; also known as Mambe. Yes, Coca is a powerful stimulant, but as an adaptogen, she also helps me chill out when needed too. At her core, however, is the ability to help us speak from a deeper place of truth. Indigenous tribes that revere her, often work with her when it's time to work out personal or tribal issues. When you have her in your system, there is no speaking falsehoods or egoic projections. She helps us communicate straight from the heart.

This downright necessity to speak truth is fitting, considering I'm owning the role of messenger right now, and it's paramount that I do so from sincere honesty. I'm so grateful to her for helping me find the courage and empowerment to write these words.

Those are just the plants I have been blessed to know in an intimate way. I've also guided people through diets with Pine, Mapacho (Tobacco), Rosemary, Cedar, Oak, Dandelion, and many more. They all have such uniquely sacred information to share, each with their own special flair and vibration.

Whatever we are seeking to understand and heal, there's a plant for that.

The Difference Between Human and Plant Consciousness

Ever wonder why plant and animal spirits give two shits about the well-being of humans when we are the ones responsible for the destruction of the planet?

Me too.

And let's be clear here, the plants are in charge. They create their own food, and reproduce on their own. They live in complete and total harmony with all that is. If we disappeared, would they actually miss us?

It turns out, some of them truly would. Ayahuasca, for one, purports to be a big fan of humanity. Yet one warm jungle afternoon, as I sat along the Amazon watching logging boats chug by, each one taking a hunk of my heart, I had to ask her why. Why on earth does she—and her plant tribe—do all they can to protect and heal us?

She answered me immediately, with her trademark wit and compassion.

Because, she told me, humans have the oh-so-hard task of owning the illusion of separateness. The universe has a way of consistently tricking itself. We humans all have egos. No other conscious entity on this planet can boast such a thing. We are literally making the unconscious, conscious. It's a big, giant, ever-evolving alchemical task. It involves pretense to separate so that we can connect with higher and higher levels of abstraction, higher and higher levels of being. And we need a hell of a lot of help. And the most profound assistance we receive comes from the spirit of the plants.

Having an ego means being immersed in the experience of duality. That's part of the magic that allows us to be wholly convinced at times that we are separate beings, and work somewhat effectively in this domain, but when we have a truly expansive spiritual aha, we remember the joke of that core wound and can feel the unification of love. Now we have evolved to work within duality without being of it! April Fools!

Plants, on the other hand, never get duped by separateness. They are forever unified albeit with a unique signature of energy and vibration for each species. Heck, every single plant has its own unique vibe. No two humans are alike, and the same is true for two lavender plants. Or two Ayahuasca vines. Or two clusters of Mushies (Magic Mushrooms).

Yet all plants are of the earth, rooted in unity, connected to the planet, and never in the experience of separateness.

The master teacher plants bow to us. They are at the ready to offer healing, insights, and love.

We just need to let them in to help us get back in touch with our true selves and our true mission, the seed of our souls. The plants aren't the only way to do so, but they most certainly are The Fast Track to this process, the adrenalized path of healing and self-discovery. When we learn about ourselves, we learn about all of consciousness. Those called to work with the Master Plants are all-in to the journey of growth and awareness.

Exactly how do we let them in? By creating and deepening a *relationship*. Just like we connect with anyone and anything.

I will describe, to the best of my ability, the indescribable; that is, what it's like to work with each of the medicines, what their superpowers consist of, as well as who they are as archetypes, elements, and the cosmic cast of characters they embody.

Come with me and let's meet the psychotropic plants.

Ayahuasca: The Mother of All Medicines

Elements: Earth, Fire
Archetypes: Ganesha, Persephone
Astrology: Pluto

Full disclosure: I am shamefully biased when it comes to Ayahuasca. She is the reason I live, breathe, dance, giggle, and get to bask in my dream life. As such, she comes first–only because it's my duty to honor her in this way.

An additional note about her complexity: The Ayahuasca I refer to is a brew made with the Ayahuasca vine (*banisteriopsis caapi*) and the leaves of Chacruna (*psychotria viridis*). There are many, many different ways to make an Aya brew, but this is the most common, and at the core of the Shipibo-Conibo tradition that I studied. We'll discuss other varieties of Ayahuasca later on.

Similarly, Ayahuasca is in the middle of a full-fledged renaissance within our western culture. I have to admit, it still astonishes me the breadth of her current net, cast literally to the ends of the earth. It's not that I doubted her power in reaching the masses, I doubted the masses' ability to work with her responsibly. And while these fears were in some ways founded, the degree to which she is welcomed and accepted by folks who have never worked with any other entheogen is utterly awe-inspiring.

She is truly Mamacita Medicina. Otherwise known as Mamahuasca.

Her superpowers as a plant spirit lie in this limitless and omnipotent capacity she holds to take us both to the depths of our psyches and to the nether regions of the multiverse. She is the medicine of duality, in that there isn't a corner of this experience she can't fling us into with unrelenting glee. She is also the medicine of multidimensional travel.

Perhaps it's fair to think of her as the queen of interdimensional frolicking—both external and internal. She is a denizen of the multiverse, and she stokes our awareness of our multidimensional selves.

For example: Her ability to be what one of my teachers called the "both and" medicine is what awes me the most. A psychedelic plant is in part identified by the ability it holds to alter our consciousness and take us on a journey. Ayahuasca has that capacity (dear deities, does she ever), but she can also take us further inside of ourselves than we've ever been before too.

If there's a place inside you that says "do not look here," she will eventually zip into that Pandora's box, and she'll do it with unadulterated joy. No apologies. Our fault for plastering a sign on the bloody cavern of secrets.

This is, of course, life-changing and empowering because repression, secrets, and lies are the stuff that suffering feeds on. Transparency is literally the key to liberation. Because we cannot hide from Ayahuasca's piercing gaze and, at times, brutal penetration into anything we are pretending not to know, she is indescribably healing.

Whatever we are hiding from, hurts us. Whatever we are conscious of, can be healed.

This is her most powerful gift to humankind. The fact that she does this with undeniable bursts of enthusiastic joy makes it either uber-insulting or terrifically entertaining, depending on your mood.

There was a night I was assisting in ceremony with my teacher, and we had a private group of just eight people sitting across from us in a squared-off circle. Aya clearly decided that this night was going to be, what I call, "Egos on parade." Every single participant went face first into wild releases of fear and pain and sadness. Purging echoed through the room, as well as fits of tears and resistance, cries for help; one woman even begged for the experience to just END ALREADY.

I started to succumb to this tempting darkness. I slipped further into my own identification with fear and suffering. And then I heard her magical little voice.

"Kat," she whispered, "These fucking fools paid for this shit!"

I giggled and gasped and quickly muffled my glee, and I instantly knew her M.O. That pulled me right out of despair and into a space where I could be of service. I'm of no use to her or anyone else if I too am getting sucked into misery.

She is wickedly funny, always having a good ole time, and witty to the max.

Did I mention she's a chatty Cathy? If you haven't worked with her or plant consciousness in general, it may seem odd to read that a plant has a penchant for verbosity. It could be that she just manifests that way for me—(the first accusation I likely ever heard as a child was that I talk too much)—but many others have described her this way to me too. In fact, a 1996 study with Psilocybin explored this very notion, noting that multiple participants spoke of experiencing a voice separate from themselves.[24] The plants communicate with us, and the deeper we fall into their portals the easier it typically is to hear them.

Before I first drank Ayahuasca in 2006, I couldn't keep a houseplant alive. So the idea that a plant might chat me up would have been

---

[24] *Listening for the Logos: A Study of Reports of Audible Voices at High Doses of Psilocybin*, Horace Beach, PhD https://maps.org/news-letters/v07n1/07112bea.html

ludicrous. Now, it's a daily reality. (No, I don't drink her every day, but I certainly connect and talk with her on the regular.)

So what is the core of her medicine? It's hard to distill her down to a single definition (the woman is literally limitless), but I will do my best.

Ayahuasca Archetypes

Ayahuasca is such a complex being, condensing her down to a single archetype is utterly impossible. Yet, think of her as the plant-based Ganesha; she is a powerhouse identifier and remover of obstacles, often symbolized by the kundalini-powered snake. She's the plant intelligence elephant in the room! She reminds me of Ganesha because of her ability to clean house; also known as La Purga, Lady Aya is aces at pushing out blockages in spiritual, mental, and physical forms. She swoops into our system, finds the toxicities and traumas that have been stored in the body and, like a spiritual jackhammer, she vibrates her consciousness through each psychic barrier until we can't hold on to that decaying piece of our journey any longer.

The purge is a fundamental element of her magic, and a core experience that frightens many curious journeyers away from her clutches. Vomiting is a mini-death and is therefore a primally feared process for many. Yet this is an essential part of her genius. Her Ganesha superpower is finding and dislodging these dense bodies of energy and poison in both our physical and energetic beings. These are the obstacles that prevent us from experiencing more joy, expansion, vitality, and light. She embodies what Rumi spoke of when he said, "Your task is not to seek for love, but merely to seek and find all the barriers within yourself that you have built against it." In Sanskrit, the word "amythyatvat" means the removal of that which is false. This describes Aya to a T.

The purge is most obviously experienced through expelling this density (called "huacha" in Quechua) into our personal buckets; a signature sight in every Aya ceremony. But purging comes in all kinds of forms, as Ganesha works in limitless ways. We can also cry, yawn, poop, shake, laugh, cough, and itch our way through this movement of energy. The visions she creates are even tied, at times, to a mental purge. In short, the woman moves energy at turbo speeds, and we do our best to surrender to this process and let her snake-like mastery heal us on all levels. It's not comfortable, but it is magical. And my goodness does it work miracles.

Another archetype central to Ayahuasca's personality is Persephone; otherwise known as the goddess of the underworld. I spent a summer on the magical island of Sicily, also known as "Persephone's Island," in part because the first mythical archetype I ever felt personally connected to was this radiant, polarizing powerhouse. Persephone is the daughter of Demeter, also known as Mother Earth. The story goes that Hades, the devil himself, lured Miss P into the underworld with a pomegranate, thereby claiming her as his wife. Demeter was so devastated to lose her daughter's presence, she began to freeze and atrophy, which, in turn, caused the earth to shrivel and fade into winter. Zeus, ever the beloved narcissist, was enraged as a frozen earth meant no crops, and therefore no food to sustain his worshippers. A god without people to worship him might as well be a mere mortal. So something had to give.

Zeus eventually worked out a deal with Hades that Persephone could spend six months in the middle world hanging with Mom and the crew, and the rest of the year as Hades' blushing bride. This is the mythological reason we have seasons; fall and winter are the times Persephone spends in hell, and spring and summer, she is back with her mom.

Here is the most striking parallel to Ayahuasca; I learned during my time in Sicily that while this tale makes Persephone sound like a damsel in distress, she is anything but. Miss P didn't just accept her fate; she made it work for her tenfold. She owned and embraced her role as the underworld queen. She learned to completely adore and embody the darkness, the same as she did the light. She made hell a bloody good time.

And that right there completely encapsulates the energy of Ayahuasca. She will take you to the depths of your demonic psyche with grace, giggles, and aplomb. The darkest nights and the most beautiful nights are equally sacred and delightful to her. And she invites us to feel the same, to mother our pains and our joys with the same amount of reverence and love.

Because of this parallel, the astrological matchup for Ayahuasca is most obviously Pluto. In our natal charts, Pluto symbolizes the energy of extremes. He shows us how we relate to birth and death and power. He is the bulldozer of fiery truth that reveals the tiniest thread of victim consciousness, and brutally reflects not only the lie inherent in this resistance to what is, but how this is the core of our suffering. The devil is just an angel in a spooky costume. Pluto shows us how we work with the energy of creation *and* destruction; since the latter is typically feared and resisted, Pluto and Ayahuasca lovingly, and relentlessly, dare us to love that, too.

Ayahuasca likes to tell me that there's a Hitler and a Mother Theresa inside each and every one of us. Culturally, we are encouraged and programmed to revere the compassionate mother, and deny, ignore, and abhor the violent villain. Yet this resistance only empowers the angry destroyer inside of us. The more we sit down and have a cup of tea with our own personal Hitlers, the more we allow the angelic energies to shine. Denial empowers the darkness. The light and love of our consciousness abate it. Just being with our own hyperbolic drive for control characteristic of a Hitler allows us to accept those aspects of ourselves rather than seeking to control them. Peace. Just being with the devotional qualities characteristic of a bhakti yogini like Mother Theresa can allow us to abide those bouts of suffering that are so inevitable and delicious. Ananda.

Everyone and everything is a reflection of consciousness, and therefore wishes to be seen, felt, and validated. That's easy-peasy if we are facing our beauty and sweetness. Confronting our fiery rage, our ability to completely annihilate ourselves and each other; that can be a devastatingly difficult process. Yet Ayahuasca knows that's where the magic lies. Making friends with the devil within is the process of understanding and integrating him. Even loving him. There is nothing more empowering.

I mentioned earlier that in October of 2017, my beloved home at the time, the deliciously polarizing city of Las Vegas, faced a terrible tragedy: The mass shooting at the Route 91 music festival. Dozens of people were killed, and hundreds were injured and traumatized. Four days later, I was in that ceremony with Madre. I had a lot to heal; while I had not lost anyone close to me, my city was in mourning, and I had been coaching people who were at the event, or on duty as a first responder, all week. I was raw and tender and frightened. I asked her to show me mercy and to help heal my heart.

The medicine was intensely strong that night. She enveloped me in the vibration of creation and destruction. Then she told me the path to healing involved a very sacred but difficult ritual; she asked me if I was up for "it." A journey into the underworld. I said yes. I told her to take me wherever she needed to.

Where she took me was so wholly unexpected, it will remain an unforgettable experience.

She led me to the hotel room of the person we assume was the sole shooter (which may or may not be true, but regardless, I understood the symbolism). I could smell the gunpowder, the stench of rage and death, as she led me through the Mandalay Bay Hotel and into his room. I stood at his feet and took in the sight of a man who had just moments before he took his own life after unleashing a fit of fury and rage onto the entire human family.

Then she said to me, "Bow to this being. Get on your knees and worship him. Give him Reiki as a show of love and support. Help this angel cross over. You do not know the horrific pain he feels. You do not get to judge him."

I did as she asked. I could never accurately describe the intensity I felt as I laid my hands on his vibrating body. But I cried tears of reverence and acceptance. I don't pretend to know the story of what really transpired that day, but regardless, I bow to and honor the perfection of consciousness. I called in the energy of Reiki, which embodies unconditional love, and I gave him every ounce of compassion I had inside of me. I did this until I felt a sense of peace wash over all of us. I sent him to the light with sacredness and love.

When we had completed this task, Ayahuasca pushed me through a psychedelic portal, and the next vision that came into view was the god of the underworld himself. He wore a white suit and had soft, pristine porcelain skin. His eyes both softly shone with blue-colored sparkles and crackled with the orange-red of an inferno. We sat down at a dainty tea table and locked eyes.

Ayahuasca let me have darshan with the devil. I remember thinking, "Brother, I see you. I love and respect you. But you can't have me. I am not on your team; I am on no one's team, except consciousness itself. But I know you are not the enemy. I know you are just the contrast we need to experience, so that we consciously get to experience love and unity."

"Hello Persephone. I see you." Those were the only words he spoke to me. But in that dance of darkness and light I saw emanating from his eyes, I felt the rest of his message. Persephone only spends half the year in hell. The other half is in heaven. But if we learn to love it all…

Hell is heaven too.

The night that followed this journey, I had the strongest satori experience to date with the medicine. I experienced eight straight hours of complete and total enlightened love; there was absolutely nothing in the multiverse that didn't have my all-in admiration and unconditional reverence and love. I didn't just get it as a mental concept, I was marinating in the truth of who we are. This is the greatest gift divinity offers.

And Ayahuasca can take us there. Back to the truth of our beingness. It can be one hell of a bumpy ride, but it's the only game in town.

When to Work With Ayahuasca

Ayahuasca is best for people who are seeking to understand themselves and the universe better. She is the most powerful medicine for shadow work, for diving into the depths of our psyches, for repressed memories, and for the healing of trauma. She's a powerhouse detoxifier, as one of her key components is the infamous purge. While not everyone purges every time, it's a common and sacred experience with her, as this is a primary way she helps move energy inside us.

Trapped energy is the stuff of future illness and current suffering. Ayahuasca has what some call Kundalini properties, and that's why we often view her as snake-like. She's like a plant medicine roto-rooter, and there is no cell inside of us, no dark corner of our awareness, that she can't eventually get to.

She's unique in the realm of psychedelics as she goes both cosmic, as most psychedelics do, as well as deeply personal and internal. If there's a "do not look here" box inside of you, Aya will find it. I can't promise when, but work with her long enough and she will get her grabby little vines in there and flip over the lid with unabandoned joy. She knows the things that hold us back are places we repress and hide from. Freedom comes through transparency, and the person we lie to the most is ourselves.

But not with Ayahuasca. Trying to hold on to a lie when you're in her clutches is about as easy as creating a square circle. It just. Doesn't. Fit.

In fact, you want to know who the hardest demographic of people I've ever worked with in ceremony is? Poker players. Not UFC fighters, not people who have been diagnosed "mentally ill," not even those with anger issues. Poker players lie for a living. They are aces at hiding the truth. As such, they can struggle like hell with Ayahuasca's illumination, and absolute requirement that self-honesty (and integrity with her) be the foundation of our union with the medicine. Fight with her around what you know to be true, and...it doesn't end well. That's the stuff of nightmares right there. And it can be very difficult to hold space for, too. Holding space is an art form we spiritual types speak of *ad nauseum*, but we don't often know what we mean when we say it. For me, it means to share an experience with someone without exhibiting an ounce of judgment or control. It means to unconditionally love and allow whatever needs to come forth to do so in safety. That's a tall order when what's coming forth is entangled in lies, self-loathing, and destruction. And yet we have to love that too if we are to understand and heal it.

The same is true for people with dark, painful repressed memories that they are simply not ready to face and accept. Whether it be the role of the victim or the perpetrator, if there isn't a conscious willingness to see and feel truth, that resistance is what can cause a full-scale psychotic break. And while these dark nights of the soul always bring profound gifts and insights, they aren't the experiences we call "good times." And they can cause a lot of trauma in the aftermath for a long, long time too, especially without aftercare support.

So she's the perfect plant partner to choose if you're ready for a big dose of illumination and integrity. She's also the obvious choice for the movement and release of energies since purging is one of her M.O.'s— in all kinds of forms. We purge physically (out both ends) to release physical toxins and ailments. We cry to release emotional trauma. We sometimes release phlegm and sweat in an intense detoxification release. We yawn and move and stretch to dislodge energies throughout our bodies. We even itch as a symbolic gesture of what we are itching to do, or get restless legs showing us what we're running from or to. And we shake like an earthquake, releasing childhood traumas. This isn't even a complete list. She's a purging, energy-releasing machine.

Go to Ayahuasca if you are ready to take all that you know and place it like a string of pearls on her altar. That is where she can show you a bigger truth. All it requires is a calling, and the manifestation of a circle that gives you the green light to participate and makes you feel safe. If you're willing to let go of the attachments and world views that are the sources of your pains and sufferings, this is the medicine that shows you the ultimate healing power of love.

The Difference Between Ayahuasca and Yagé

The world of Ayahuasca can be a very confusing place as there are dozens of traditions and an endless number of ways to make the brew. The most common contrast is between Ayahuasca and a brew called Yagé. Ayahuasca and Yagé are names that sometimes refer to the same combination of plants, and other times reference two entirely different teas. Yes, it's confusing!

Yagé most commonly refers to the Colombian lineage of Ayahuasca usage. Some tribes in Ecuador call the brew Yagé as well. Those tribes typically use the same components in the brew—that is, the Ayahuasca vine and the Chacruna leaves. This marriage creates the magic of the medicine. One without the other is a subtle, almost indiscernible experience. Together, they are the portal of this profoundly powerful altered state.

Ecuadorian Yagé is often prepared differently; while the Peruvian Ayahuasca takes the entire vine and mashes it for the brew, some tribes in Ecuador strip the bark and use only the woody center. Colombian Yagé, however, typically utilizes a very different DMT component called Chaliponga instead of Chacruna. While Chaliponga contains the same familiar DMT alkaloid as Chacruna (used for the out-of-body experience), the personalities of these plants are so vastly different that they are considered two entirely separate plant spirits.

Although I am an experienced Ayahuasquera and I have drunk Yagé many times, I would have absolutely no idea how to lead a Yagé ceremony. Brewmasters who make Yagé do so with different techniques and prayers, and every step in the process changes the vibration of the medicine. Furthermore, Yagé ceremonies differ from Ayahuasca circles in that they are typically all night events—from sunset to sunrise. They use different music, different methods of healing, and different tools and techniques.

This all speaks to the complexity and variations of the medicine, and the nuances involved in leading ceremonies. In other words, a shaman trained in the Shipibo tradition of pouring Ayahuasca in no way implies the know-how and experience to pour Yagé in the Colombia lineage. These plants are so immensely multifaceted, a practitioner normally will only have the time to focus on two or three plants as a carrier in their entire lifetime. So, if someone proclaims that Ayahuasca is Ayahuasca, they are badly misinformed. Each step and touchpoint in the process matters. Ask any pizza aficionado if "pizza is pizza," and you'll get a passionate and rousing response about how the flour, the sauce/cheese/toppings ratio, and even the water in the dough deeply matter. The same is true for plant medicine brews. Not to mention the love and intentions a brewmaster puts into his or her creation.

Yagé as a medicine has more of the embodiment of the marriage of divine feminine and masculine than traditional Ayahuasca, simply because Chaliponga is an overtly masculine plant. The experience has a more decidedly direct and masculine approach, with profoundly deep meditation qualities, as well as purification. A Yagé ceremony is an all-night celestial party, but it's far, far more purgative than Aya as well. The most identifiable part of a Yagé ceremony is often the lineup in front of the bathroom; this is a medicine that will clean out every last cell in your body and take you on a journey through the cosmos.

As a receiver of the medicines, it's a beautiful experience to try various traditions and brews to find what resonates most with each individual.

As long as you are sitting with experienced, safe, and reverent leaders, wherever you are called to experience the medicine's magic is divine.

DMT vs. Ayahuasca: Flying Without a Pilot

DMT—or Dimethyltryptamine—is the component in Chacruna (and Mimosa, etc.) that creates the out-of-body, uber-altered experience that Ayahuasca is famous for. Many are big fans of working with an isolated, chemically extracted DMT. I'm here to sound the alarm that this is in no way the same as working with Aya, and if you're asking a humble servant of the plants whether or not it's a good idea, my answer is a resounding *no* in almost all cases.

I encounter folks on the regular that have a rabid love of journeying with DMT. Many come to ceremony with dozens of DMT journeys under their belts, expecting to have a similar experience with Ayahuasca. So let me be perfectly clear: If all you know is DMT, you do not know Ayahuasca. DMT is to Aya what Cocaine is to Coca. That is, they are not at all in the same ballpark. Here's why.

Extracting a single alkaloid from any complex plant structure does not honor the consciousness and wholeness of the plant. If you extracted just my personal proclivity for talking up a storm, you would not have a clue that I am at times exceedingly introverted and highly introspective. Therefore, the separation of one aspect of a plant's potency does not even begin to give you a full understanding of that consciousness. Just ask Cannabis. When we extract out only her THC, we know nothing of the healing power of other cannabinoids like CBD and various subsets. Plants are just as complex as we are. Maybe even more so.

Furthermore, let me go on record as saying the recreational DMT usage is not only disrespectful, but also outright dangerous. Smoking or vaping DMT is like skydiving without a parachute. Sure, it might be a fun adventure, and just maybe you'll discover a safety net, but there's a good chance you'll crash and burn. Even more dicey, you might not know it until you've manifested multiple challenging reflections that you don't even know are connected to the unconscious usage of DMT.

Back in the early days of my love affair with Ayahuasca, a dear friend, who is a bit of an alchemist, perfected the art of extracting DMT from the Mimosa plant. I embarked on many a journey, at first in a more recreational way, and later in a more intentional and sacred way. By and large, my journeys were beautiful and deep and multidimensional.

Yet I couldn't help but notice a decided difference between the fifteen-minute DMT cosmic explorations and the six-hour deep dives with Mama Ayahuasca. One was decidedly more mental, the other deeply felt. One was a blast off into the multiverse, the other a journey both inward and outward, full of discomfort and purging and difficulties. But the latter was actually healing. Deeply, profoundly transforming. While DMT did have things to teach me about consciousness and our role within it, there was no tour guide. Ayahuasca was not there to drive the spaceship, and through careful witnessing of my own journeys and of those who came to ceremony with lots of DMT experience under their belts, I began to see a bigger story unfold.

People who love DMT are quite often very defensive about this habit. That's the first sign that perhaps there's more to the story. There was a gentleman that came to sit with my teacher and I, many years ago, that was the catalyst to my awakening with the dangers of DMT. He was a sweet soul, very intelligent, but had been heavily using DMT. He was battling a serious rage addiction, finding himself lashing out at random times, sometimes so blindly full of anger that he would black out and lose awareness of his words and actions. He came to Aya for healing and insight.

What I saw that night absolutely derailed me. As he purged, streams of dark energies and entities came flowing out of him. Aya was there with me, narrating what I was witnessing. This is when she first schooled me about DMT.

DMT, she told me, is a complete dishonoring of the plants from which it is extracted from. It's like using a woman for her body, without acknowledging or honoring the whole person. It's a violation, and there are definitely repercussions. These almost never show up immediately in the actual DMT experience. That would be too obvious and convenient. No, this karma shows up in various aspects of lives, rather mysteriously, but still ever-present. For the soul mentioned above, it manifested as anger. For others, it manifests as illness, sadness, confusion, and always unconsciousness.

That last piece is the key to the puzzle: Unconsciousness. Those who do earnest work with plant medicines and truly integrate those experiences, become more conscious over time. Those that recreationally abuse elements extracted from plants do the opposite.

And if you fall into the latter category, I suspect you're already crafting the angry email or response to this accusation. Please don't bother, as you will only be proving this point. It's not unanimous, I know there are exceptions, but why fly a plane without a pilot when the sacredness of the medicine itself is so much more powerful, alive, and healing?

Most of us don't have the faintest idea about the spiritual world, but that doesn't mean it doesn't exist. Many who abuse substances like DMT insist it's just an innocent experience of an altered consciousness. But what you don't know *can* actually hurt you.

The spirit world is just as complex as our tangible one. And if we don't know how to create a safe container for ourselves, we are flypaper to the myriad of energies. What are these energies exactly? That's part of the mystery, but think of the spirit world like the human one; some folks have wonderful vibrations and energies, others feel dark, heavy, and delusional. Spirits are the same. Some of these energies feel immensely uplifting and expansive, others feel terrifying, confusing, and even traumatic or harmful. This is precisely why we need protection.

It isn't always obvious when we pick up a hitchhiker energy either, so this is very tricky business indeed. Take the gentleman I referenced above. He was working with DMT regularly, having a good ole time in the cosmos. It never occurred to him that his increased issues with rage and instability might be related. But substances like DMT completely crack us open; we become staggeringly vulnerable and often unaware of how energies might swoop in and start feeding on our life force.

This all sounded very far-fetched to me once upon a time too. But after witnessing the ramifications of unconscious and unsafe altered spaces, there is no longer an ounce of doubt inside of me. Couple this with the awareness that plants require our reverence and discernment, in part to honor them and in part to honor us, and it's clear that "fun times on drugs" can result in painful karmic lessons.

Everything I wrote above is my experience and, as with anything in the spiritual space, it's a perspective, not an Absolute Truth. I can certainly hold that there is a way to be conscious, respectful, and sacred about working with DMT. This is hardly the norm, however, but I honor those that break the mold. Just don't let these exceptions fool you into thinking you qualify if you're not mindful of creating a protected container and staying in deep communication with the plants themselves. Neither ignorance nor arrogance can protect us. Listening, awareness, and reverence do.

If you have a connected relationship with plants like Mimosa or Chacruna, and you work with them as partners to extract their medicines and seek their wisdom, good on you. But if you're doing this with any ounce of egotistic desires, agendas, or lack of awareness, there will be repercussions.

I, personally, have zero desire to work with a chemical extraction when the plant itself is so alive, so powerful, so protective and wise. I prefer to imbibe with a spiritual being, not a synthetic or manipulated substance. But all roads lead to awakening, and anything can be sacred—as long as we make the effort to treat it that way.

Papa Iboga: The Tribal Medicine of Empowerment

Elements: Earth, Air
Archetypes: Mebeghe, Shiva
Astrology: Saturn

From the wild and forested region of Gabon in West Africa comes Iboga, another mystical, enormously powerful master plant that has been used for thousands of years in healing rituals. Iboga has been cultivated and protected by the Bwiti tribe, and the Bwiti still lead and train others to work with this powerhouse. Iboga is arguably the most potent, masculine, intensely difficult plant medicine in the world. His ceremonies last at least 12 hours, with aftereffects lasting up to several weeks after a single dose. He is so challenging to work with that practitioners normally only have a dozen or so ceremonies in their lifetime; and unlike Ayahuasca, an Iboga shaman does not take the same large dose of medicine participants do when they are leading the way. Iboga requires restraint, profound reverence, and many, many years of study before anyone can accurately proclaim themselves a true partner.

While I have personally never been called to work with Iboga, and therefore have never consumed him, I am very close to many who know him well. I was also visited by Papa Iboga once in an Ayahuasca ceremony; I had been sitting next to a gentleman who had worked with him extensively for healing, and as such, received a surprise yet unforgettable visit. He appeared to me as a massive, overtly masculine face carved in the trunk of a tree. His presence completely hijacked my journey and I was awestruck and frightened. Since I didn't recognize him at first, I asked him to identify himself. In the most baritone, booming voice, he told me his name. "I am EEEEE-BO-GAHHHHH!" He brought in a gaggle of his indigenous guardians and they danced manically around me. I bowed and cowered in his magnificent presence, tears rolling down my face as I witnessed his omnipotence. It was an honor to have just this glimpse of his consciousness, and he disappeared as fast as he swooped in. This powerful flash is all I have needed to know what a force he is, and to have the sincerest humility and respect for his medicine.

Iboga is a bona fide wild child, ancient as all get out, completely and equally aligned with darkness and light, and not a plant to be taken with any amount of casualness. Yet he holds masterful superpowers unmatched by any other entheogen, and is one of the most controversial ones too.

When one is called to Iboga, they are called to far more than just a plant, but to an entire cultural tradition and a full-scale spiritual journey. Iboga's superpowers are many, but they mostly encompass healing ancestral wounds, taking people through intensely beautiful shadow work experiences via the masculine perspective (which often involves processing anger, abuse, fear, trauma, and depression), and the incredible experience of a life review. Iboga is famous for giving participants the 30,000-foot view of their lives, much like a near-death experience can trigger when we take stock in our experiences and choices from an expanded perspective.

Papa Iboga is pure mind medicine; he clears out the clutter of lies and stories and helps people get to the heart of what is true for them and who they want to be. He's a massive dose of empowerment, teaching all those who walk with him how to show up in their fire and fierceness, and he can often tap into repressed memories or forgotten dreams. He is an incredible tool for self-discovery, for bursting through feelings of stagnation and confusion, and he's ideal for anyone who needs to feel their divine masculine strength.

Iboga is perhaps most famous for dealing with the prevalent issues of addiction in all its shadowy forms. One of his most potent alkaloids, Ibogaine, is regularly extracted solely for administering to addicts. While this is immensely effective, it's also wildly controversial. So let's take a deep dive into the polarity of using Ibogaine to heal the worst of our society's dysfunctions.

The Ethics and Power of Ibogaine

On the plus side, pure Ibogaine is an absolute godsend to humanity that can literally be a healing catalyst for even the most horrendous addictions. People suffering from opiate and alcohol abuse have experienced miraculous resets from Ibogaine, as it has the power to put an addict's neurochemistry back to a pre-addicted state within 45 minutes of receiving a flood dose. Ibogaine can help move through Post-Acute Withdrawal Symptoms, also known as P.A.W.S., in a single session; these are the cravings that send people back to the throes of their addiction in the aftermath of a detox. Depending on a person's metabolism, this can last for 1-3 months, which gives ample time for the individual to change their lifestyle and ground-in to sobriety. Ibogaine has taken thousands of people from the brink of death and destruction back to normalcy and empowerment.

Yet there is a cost, and it's a fascinating industry. The world of ibogaine attracts a decidedly masculine archetype, and many are jumping on the healing train for profit, not healing, due to the potential far-reaching effects the pandemic of opiate addiction holds. Unlike Ayahuasca, many of the doctors and quasi-doctors that are stepping forth to administer Ibogaine have zero experience with the plant itself. This is partly because Iboga is so bloody powerful and intimidating. He is also not a plant that the facilitator can work with while holding space; he's far too altering to focus on anything other than the journey itself. But the most prevalent reason many people do not develop a mutual relationship with Iboga before working with Ibogaine lies in the Western disease of ignorance and greed. There are many tragic stories for the people involved in the Ibogaine business—so many, in fact, that it points to the reality that this plant is not fond of being disrespected, and he will strike back. Mysterious accidents like fatal car crashes and sudden deaths, as well as various other traumas, befall many unsuspecting people working with Ibogaine purely for profit. Very few people have been able to achieve any substantial level of success thus far, despite the potential gains. Many clinics have also been shut down by legal authorities in places like Mexico and the U.S. So while there are tremendous benefits and potential successes available with Ibogaine, the obstacles seem endless as well.

However, Ibogaine is also experiencing its own renaissance, partly because there are so many millions of people that need legitimate addiction therapy. The average success rate at a traditional rehab for opiate addiction (success equating to a full year of sobriety after treatment) is roughly 4% (and in some cases, that's a generous figure). For experienced Ibogaine clinics, that rate can soar to 60% or more.[25] This is exceptionally powerful medicine.

There are multiple complications as to why this world is so polarizing. To begin with, there are only a handful of countries where Iboga and

---

[25] https://clearskyibogaine.com/ibogaine-treatment-success-rate

Ibogaine are currently legal or decriminalized. Places like Costa Rica, Portugal, and Australia all have some level of legal tolerance, as does Mexico, home of the highest present-day concentration of Ibogaine clinics. Legally speaking, however, the laws that govern these substances are gray areas at best, and clinics are shut down just as fast as they are opened sometimes, leaving the landscape a confusing one to decipher.

Most poignantly, however, the issue of safety and ethics fiercely plagues this plant in a tangible way. Iboga and Ibogaine are the most dangerous of the psychotropics. Ibogaine in particular has the power to cause cardiac arrest, and many have perished seeking treatment. This means Ibogaine should never be used in a psycho-spiritual ceremony but instead needs to be administered in clinics that must be run like hospitals, not retreats. Of course, not everyone has the integrity to honor this necessity, and when people without traditional medical training purport to be experts in the process, the results can be deadly. Even in a controlled and experienced setting, heart complications and deaths occur.

Ethically speaking, it's not fair to just blame the power of the plant for these health risks. The people seeking Ibogaine often have bodies ravaged by years of severe opiate abuse, which can also cause significant heart and liver damage. A reputable Ibogaine clinic will do a full heart, lung, and liver panel for every patient before issuing a flood dose, thereby ensuring the highest possibility of safety and success. But this process is not regulated, and so many clinics lure in clients without legitimately promising their safety. With a pandemic of addiction, there's a lot of money at stake in the world of Ibogaine, and corners are constantly cut. This thereby gives the plant a bad name, when really it's the reckless and egocentric people that own the fault of harm.

Finally, Iboga suffers from the issue of availability. The roots of Iboga are where the medicine resides, and it takes a minimum of seven years to reach full maturity. Because of the far-reaching effects of opiate and alcohol addiction, Iboga has been severely deforested. There are no current definitive statistics, but it is widely believed that very little Iboga still exists in the wild. The Bwiti tribe, the indigenous people who have used Iboga for hundreds of years in sacred ceremonies, are even now reportedly using alcohol instead of Iboga in their rituals. This has obvious tragic consequences.

From my knowledge of plant spirit communication, it is my educated speculation that the Ibogaine world is teeming with tragedy and conflict because many of the people who get involved do not understand the dynamics and ethics of working with a powerful psychotropic. Iboga is a living, conscious entity, and he is being disrespected and misused for personal gain. As a result, there are serious consequences befalling many who have acted out of alignment, whether from ignorance or greed. And these results are just beginning to surface.

In the meantime, because of the scarcity of the medicine, many are guilty of illegally poaching resources from Africa to meet the needs of their clients and clinics. Yet the average person seeking help holds little to no awareness of all this ethical drama.

The bottom line is that Iboga is a partner for helping to solve one of the most tragic and deadly problems our global culture faces, but he won't be around much longer to offer healing if we do not learn to be a respectful partner with him. Opiate addiction is now the leading cause of death in North America for people under the age of 50, even more deadly than car accidents.[26] So, on the one hand, a tangible solution is desperately needed, and his success rates are completely untouched by any other method.

On the other hand, we as humans need to establish a much more aligned and reverent relationship with the Earth as a whole and with Iboga as a spiritual partner, or we won't have any medicine left with which to aid in addiction recovery.

Furthermore, as a global culture, we desperately need to work out the actual repercussions and ethics of extracting a singular alkaloid from a conscious being. It makes sense why humans do this with Iboga, as using the plant in its natural form does not offer enough Ibogaine saturation to reset an addict's neurochemistry. This is why extraction is advocated and necessary for those on the brink of death. But because we haven't previously held that Iboga is a conscious entity, we haven't done the work to substantially study what the consequences really are.

Some are working around this issue by synthesizing Ibogaine in a laboratory, which is in essence the creation of a pharmaceutical version of the alkaloid. While this solves the issue of availability, we have now reverted straight back to what is arguably the core issue in our health industry; the idea that humans can replicate the power of plants, without repercussions. This perspective also perpetuates our horrendous disconnect from the natural world.

The truth is that all pharmaceuticals are based on plant medicines in some way; created for profit since plants cannot be patented and therefore offer more limited revenues. And yet I don't need to convince

---

26 Schiller EY, Goyal A, Mechanic OJ. *Opioid Overdose.* 2020 Nov 20. In: StatPearls [Internet]. Treasure Island (FL): StatPearls Publishing; 2021 Jan— . PMID: 29262202. https://pubmed.ncbi.nlm.nih.gov/29262202

anyone these days that the process of manufacturing health has resulted in a tremendous disconnect from our planet, who is the source of all our food, medicine, and well-being. Every drug has some level of a nightmarish list of side effects. While a synthetic form of Ibogaine may indeed duplicate some of the powerful healing effects of Iboga, there will no doubt be plenty of negative side effects that may render the entire process a failure. Yet with the limited natural resources, it's an almost impossible avoidance. So many people need and deserve the help that Ibogaine offers, but at what cost if it perpetuates our disconnect from the Earth? Does it really offer long-term healing? It's a complicated, painful, and extremely important debate.

Iboga is mirroring both our global issues with addiction, as well as our extreme disconnect from the consciousness of our planet. He is single-handedly bringing about the hope and promise for helping what is truly the worst pandemic our world faces each day—the horrific reality of addiction, not a relatively short-lived virus. Iboga also points to the accountability we have as a species for the tremendous dis-ease caused by the abuse and disregard of our planetary home, and each other.

I don't offer an easy answer, but I do trust this is a divine orchestration, and our willingness to own this shadow and see the magic of nature's healing ability is the light that will bring us to a collective solution. Our current priority must be a commitment to preserving and protecting the remaining Iboga plants, as well as the continued study and understanding of how he is a remedy for addiction. This is critical, not just in a chemical and physical sense, but in illuminating the spiritual crisis he mirrors around our relationship with our surroundings. That is arguably the root cause of much of our suffering and breakdown; we do not live in harmony with the home that feeds and heals us, and that alone causes much of our existential pain. By taking that as seriously as we do a virus like COVID-19, we actually stand a chance of healing and awakening on a global level. Papa Iboga, we bow to you.

Iboga Archetypes

The number one deity Iboga is directly tied to goes by the name of Mebeghe.[27,28] This is the creator god in the Bwiti tradition, the true carriers of Iboga. To manifest a human, all Mebeghe needs is a piece of hair, a brain cell, and a pebble from the sea. A little puff from his breath creates a cosmic egg. The egg is then gifted to a spider to hang from her web, between the sky and the sea, and the force of the sun gives life to the egg.

Papa Iboga is the ultimate masculine destroyer, and so parallels to the famous Hindu god Shiva are an obvious match as well. Shiva embodies both creation and destruction—two sides of the same life force coin— and therefore symbolize Iboga's ability to destroy an ego, giving birth to a deeper, more heart-centered awareness. Shiva's third eye, which they say has the power to literally burn karma, matches the power of Iboga to clean ancestral trauma and a lifetime of addiction, and the associated karmic repercussions. Shiva is also an avid dancer, even at what we might call inappropriate times, which draws to mind the wild music that is always a backdrop to a traditional Iboga ceremony. The Bwiti's ceremonial soundtrack is full of intensely chaotic rhythms, created in part to completely scramble our cognitive control, so that Papa Iboga can dance upon our ignorance and expand it into enlightenment.

---

[27] https://www.godchecker.com/african-mythology/MEBEGHE
[28] https://ibogainedossier.com/barabe.html

From an astrological perspective, Iboga represents Saturn. In our birth charts, Saturn points to our relationship with the sharp blade of truth and integrity, boundaries and beliefs. Like Iboga, Saturn is ruthless and wild with his lessons, showing us the obstacles and challenges we grapple with in order to surrender into the reality of who we are and our place in the greater whole. He never coddles, and he doesn't care if what he has to reflect to us is difficult or painful. His only mission is to directly display the lessons we came to learn, and to show us experientially how we still hold on to our ignorance. Iboga is the same. His love comes through intensity and directness, and if we are not ready for a harsh yet honest reflection of our blockages and resistance, then dancing with him can be enormously difficult; even traumatic. But his divinely masculine, big-picture view is relentless because, like Saturn, he does not tolerate any attempt to hide from the light of reality.

If you're called to the most ancient, direct, and intensely beautiful experience of truth, Iboga is divinely beautiful medicine. But don't jump into his arms if you're looking for soft coddling and a gentle reveal. Go to him when it's time to really Know.

When to Work With Iboga

Like any of the entheogenic plants, one is called from a deeply felt place to sit with a powerhouse like Iboga. He is a go-to for people looking to unlock the seat of their empowerment, and is a beautiful medicine when you're ready to do shadow work on yourself and your lineage, especially on the father's side. He is also ideal for people with a physical or spiritual connection to the West African heritage he embodies, and is therefore most advantageous for ceremonial usage in his home in Gabon. There are reputable and loving places in Costa Rica and elsewhere for ceremonial use of Iboga, but if you really want to know him, it doesn't get any more powerful than visiting his home.

Iboga is amazing mind medicine; it can clear out the clutter and cobwebs and help actualize the power of a focused and aligned mind. He is a beautiful medicine for healing trauma, especially if caused by masculine forces. Many also report that Iboga is a master cleanser of viral infections, nerve disorders, chronic fatigue, autoimmune disorders, and the general feeling of malaise. He creates an experience of "life review" where one is allowed to witness their past experiences in a more expanded and detached way, thereby giving broader perspective to the divinity of traumatic occurrences and bringing about a tremendous sense of forgiveness and peace.

Perhaps Iboga's most profound gift, in addition to his superpowers with addiction, is the opportunity to experience an egoless state. He has the ability to completely quiet the monkey mind that wants to own the seat of identity, and like Ayahuasca, can offer participants a chance to be consciously connected to source without that false self. In other words, a deep experience with Iboga can remind us of who we really are, in a deeply felt and conscious sense.

Huachuma: The Heavy Feather and the Golden Chalice

Elements: Fire, Air
Archetypes: Saint Peter, Apollo, Ra, Yoda
Astrology: Sun

If you've ever had the sacred experience of sitting on a back porch with your grandfather, gracefully poised on rocking chairs while looking at the night sky and conversing about the hidden mysteries, you have an idea of how it feels to merge with Grandfather Cactus.

Huachuma, also known as San Pedro (Latin name *echinopsis pachanoi*), is a sacred medicine born from the Andes of South America. There are a few lineages that have practiced the art of ceremony with him for thousands of years, including the Q'ero and Chavin traditions. The latter is the path I fell into almost fifteen years ago, and it's a path that was literally almost lost until my mentor and teacher, Howard Lawler, magically brought it back into our modern day awareness. The tiny village of Chavin, located way up in the mountains in western Peru, is home to the sacred Chavin de Huantar temple, the underground creation devoted to the almighty jaguar. This was home to countless Huachuma ceremonies dating back to 1200 BC, which makes this the oldest recorded psychotropic medicine.

Huachuma is life-force energy, just like the cactus he comes from, which can grow several stories tall in his effort to pierce the sun. The main alkaloid in Huachuma is mescaline, which also holds the distinction of being the first substance coined "psychedelic" by Aldous Huxley in 1954. Some consider cactus medicine to be the greatest teacher of all because his mission is to bring us back to wholeness, unity, and the experience of unconditional love.

In many ways, Huachuma is the trickiest to work with, as he is anything but direct and contained. Like a good grandfather, he breaks all the rules and requires patience and reverence to access his secrets. But since they are the most sacred lessons of all about our eternal connection to source, everything he asks for is worth it, times infinity.

Many have tried to make his medicine with efficacy and potency, heading to the local nursery and coming home with a few cactus to plop on the stove and brew. If you read the hundreds of internet threads about the process of making his medicine, you'll find it's littered with complexity, as well as many frustrated accounts that hours were spent to make a medicine and "nothing really happened." This isn't because Huachuma is weak or even subtle; he just operates very differently than his psychotropic friends. Grandpa makes us work for it. We have to meet him halfway.

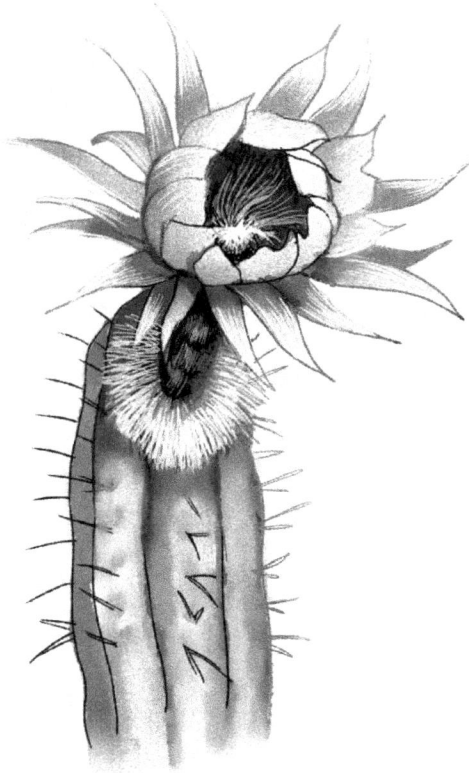

What this means is that if we are not making his medicine from a place of humility and love, he is often not deeply felt at all. He is not the sledgehammer that Iboga and Ayahuasca can masquerade as; Howard always told me Huachuma is a mighty feather. He can be soft and gentle in his power, or wield the feather like a sword. But he does not bend to our desire to have "fun times on drugs." Grandfather will protect and teach those that go to him with this request by creating an experience too subtle to really ascertain. But those that know to approach him as the holiest of holy... well, he'll give us the keys to the kingdom.

Mine has been an extraordinarily blessed path with this beloved medicine. I accidentally landed in the hands of the most revered and powerful living Huachumero when I first felt the calling to drink Ayahuasca. Howard Lawler is thought to have single-handedly brought back the Chavin tradition of working with Huachuma, and since he owned the Ayahuasca lodge I first went to for shamanic healing, I struck a deep friendship with him right out of the gate. I didn't know for a couple of years how special and powerful he was; not until I accepted his many requests and offerings to experience his magical medicine.

My first journey with Grandfather Cactus happened in the jungle, at Howard's SpiritQuest Lodge. He offered any participants that wanted to stay after an Ayahuasca cycle the chance to work with Huachuma in an introductory way. Howard taught me that it's rather essential for folks called to Huachuma to first work with Mama Aya since she takes us within and helps us clean out toxins and resistance and emotional trauma. Huachuma can bookend her magic by taking us home to our hearts. Working with cactus first before we've done any shadow work with a plant such as Ayahuasca, is premature at best, and insanely disappointing or difficult at worst. Howard taught me that we must first understand the darkness with Madre, and then Grandpa lets us discover the power of the light.

My first dance with the cactus transformed me. At the head of a Huachuma ceremony lies the altar, or "la mesa" as the tradition calls it. Howard's was utterly spectacular. To the left, the shaman places all items that connect to death and the underworld, to the right goes the upper-world tools—all those objects connected to the light—and in the center, called the "axis mundi," goes the practitioner's most sacred tools. Howard had a massive jaguar skull straight down the middle of his mesa, and it sucked me into a portal of timelessness and magic. The objects on the altar literally come alive when one is deep in the clutches of cactus, and I stood for hours at Howard's mesa over the years, letting each holy item teach me lessons of empowerment, connection, and love.

Over the years, I had the incredible privilege and honor of attending multiple events with Howard; journeys he called "Pilgrimages Through Time." He would take his assembled tribe all through northern Peru, visiting sacred sites built thousands of years ago for the sole purpose of convening with cactus. Each of the five temples or holy places we would visit held an absolutely beautiful vortex of history and energy, and each place had an incredible story to tell. Every time I joined him for the journey, the relationship with these places of power would deepen, and more universal truths would be revealed by Huachuma and these earthly spaces that held his vitality and wisdom.

Howard isn't here any longer, and for now, those journeys are not available, so my privilege of knowing and working with him feels almost unreal. The honor of walking with him in this capacity is one of the core reasons I have wanted to pen this book for many, many years. We used to sit around in our post-Huachuma vibrations, talking about the state of the world, and he would always tell me to write this book; that I was part of the messenger crew with the duty and honor of being a voice for the plants. He wanted the knowledge he was able to echo into the tangible world via his beloved cactus to be shared as loud and wide as it could possibly reach, because the intelligence of this plant holds the truths we need to expand and evolve as a species.

Howard wasn't just a white dude that traveled to South America and fell in love with the traditions and medicines; he embodied the spirit of an authentic shaman. He lived in Peru for several decades, married an amazing Peruvian woman, and built a highly respected and truly spectacular medicine retreat that came way before the big influx of Ayahuasca tourism. Howard lived and breathed the shamanic path. The locals called him "Ortorongo Blanco," which means "The White Jaguar" due to his shock of white hair and fierce yet friendly demeanor. I found the real deal from the word go, and I'll never stop giving gratitude to this Maestro.

So while Ayahuasca takes us on a cosmic journey of self-discovery through the underworld and through our own psyches, San Pedro awakens the wisdom inside of us that knows everything is always OK. I can't think of a message the world needs to feel and know with any more urgency. I promise you, if the whole world had a chance to know Huachuma the way Howard let his pilgrims experience him, there would be no violence, no war, no planetary destruction.

I have been lucky enough to not only visit many sacred sites, but to do so under the influence of the plant medicine they honor. I have two favorites to share; these are profoundly special temples that hold the vibrations of the thousands of rituals that have occurred over just as many years, and if you ever have the opportunity to visit one, it will become undeniable that each holds palpable magic.

The first sacred site is called El Brujo, and it's along the northern coast of Peru. The Moche or Mochita civilization built this duo of temples near present-day Trujillo between the years 100-700 AD. The remains still exist today, and archaeologists have been excavating one of the temples for many years now. The pyramids were referenced as the Life

Giving and the Life Taking temples, which is reflective of how they were used in rituals during the tribe's existence.

I have done multiple Huachuma journeys here, which was their medicine of choice too. We begin by drinking the sacrament along the coast, and what's notable and magical about the area is the constant existence of two wind systems that come together in a perpendicular fashion, creating a sound effect that sounds like a gaggle of helicopters. The first time the medicine came on for me in this location, I kept looking for the source of that incredible noise, only to discover it was the wind, and it's *always* blowing in this fashion here. This is precisely why the Moche built the Life Giving huaca (temple) in this spot. The energy is off the charts magical, full of life force and empowerment and the unmistakable feeling of being truly alive. Obviously, you need to experience this sound to truly grok it, but sound healers and engineers like Sufi Hazrat Inayat Khan also offer a complementary framework for understanding this modality of healing.

But it gets even more delicious. The temple here embodies the energy of the divine feminine. They built the temple for sex rituals aimed at the fertility gods, and it was a sacred place for the tribe to honor the process of creating and giving life. No one is allowed in the temple anymore, and it's been eroded into more of a mound than a pyramid, with a slit down the center carved by the intense winds that have made it look like—you guessed it—a vagina.

Back in the day, we were allowed to climb to the top of this structure, and words could never begin to describe the amazing feminine vibration we all felt as we rolled around in the dirt, soaking up the euphoric vibrations. The first time I visited El Brujo, every single woman in our crew of 11 menstruated at the top of the huaca, including a woman who had been in menopause for 19 years. Yes, it's that powerful. I wasn't due to bleed for two weeks, and my body had a massive release. I felt giddy, so incredibly womanly, and drunk on all of creation. While the men obviously didn't get the benefit of an awakened uterus, they felt equally punch-drunk and joyful; all of us were like school kids set loose in an opulent bouncy house.

Off in the distance, about a mile walk, a very ominous temple stands waiting. This is the Life Taking huaca. The Moche used this for intentional human sacrifice in order to appease the weather gods responsible for bringing El Niño to their lands every couple of decades or so, which would kill a large number of their people. So this temple, which is built in an area where there is no wind, no movement, no sound—an eerie contrast to the wildness of the feminine—is a remaining sacred site where many lost their lives for the greater good of the tribe. The Moche shamans discovered that these occasional sacrificial rituals, executed as offerings to the deities, would indeed curb the devastation of El Niño. But, in typical human fashion, they didn't stop exploring their power once they found out how to control the weather.

Visiting that temple in the peak of a Huachuma experience is the most humbling yet horrifying experience of power I have ever known. Our Huachumero called it the "dark side of heaven," and it brought on the most difficult journey I've ever had with this divine cactus brew.

When I first visited El Brujo, there was a legend the locals told of the Moche's most powerful sorceress—a young woman who died in her twenties but remained the Moche's most revered shaman. Years later, when I returned, they had discovered her remains. She's known as the Lady of Cao, and it is believed her mummified remains are so powerful, we are not allowed to look directly at her; instead they've created a museum and have only her reflection on display.[29]

I have viewed her reflection multiple times while deep with Huachuma and I can tell you she exudes beauty and divine power. By studying all her jewelry and leaning into her energies, my estimation is that she was so powerful because she wholly embraced all of duality. The Lady of Cao likely did not decipher between darkness and light, good and evil—she vibrated in the knowingness that it's all sacred, it's all God-stuff, and nothing is to be feared, controlled, or contained.

She was and is still an immense teacher for me. I have used her image and energy as a guide when I navigate the darkness many times, and I will likely always continue to do so. To view her in any state of consciousness is an incredible blessing. She is, to me, the poster child for what shamanism encapsulates. She embodies the idea that shamanism is a passage beyond life and death, good and evil, and all of duality. It is the bridge to unity, and we have the invitation to experience life as such even while we're here, immersed in contrast.

My second example is my favorite place in the entire world. It's called Chavin, located high up in the Peruvian Andes, and it's a village untouched by time or western culture. There's an underground mecca there called The Temple of the Jaguar. It's built using sacred geometry at the headwaters of the Amazon River, and in between the glorious Cordillera Negra and Cordillera Blanca mountain ranges (Black and White). The Chavin culture built this temple some 3,000 years ago, and it's by far the holiest site for lovers of Huachuma.

---

[29] Mummipedia Wiki, Lady of Cao, https://mummipedia.fandom.com/wiki/Lady_of_Cao

Chavin means "center of the center" in Quechua, and at the center of this temple lies a sculpture called the Lanzon. Once again I can't even begin to find language that accurately describes what it's like to be deep with cactus medicine and witnessing the holiest of the holy, but I can say simply that viewing this intricately carved art piece is very much like viewing God in a rock. It absolutely vibrates with enlightenment; this radiant, pure, immaculately perfect energy exudes from every groove. I have been here multiple times and I always leave dumbstruck, humbled, tearful, and completely heart-centered. You know that feeling you have when you're deep in nature and you can feel the connectedness and consciousness of every speck of dirt, every animal, every rock and plant? Yes, just like that. There are vortexes on this planet that are like portals into higher awareness, and Chavin is one of them, hence the temple. In America, places like Sedona, AZ, Asheville, SC, and Moab, UT hold similar sacred energies.

No one really knows how the Chavin people were able to carve perfectly symmetrical, mind-blowingly beautiful creations in stone—they are flawless, and even more potent is that sublime energy that radiates from every piece. Picasso was deeply inspired by Chavin artwork too; you can easily see the inspiration in his masterful works.[30]

Most importantly, Chavin remains the ultimate pilgrimage for people who resonate with the medicine of Huachuma. There are Peruvian Torch and San Pedro cactuses standing on guard throughout the temple, and it's the perfect example of a pristine shamanic vortex that we still have the immense honor of visiting. It's a schlep to get there—

---

[30] *The Ceramic Plates of Pablo Picasso: A Master of Form,*
https://news.masterworksfineart.com/2019/06/07/the-ceramic-plates-of-pablo-picasso-a-master-of-form

you really have to work for it—but that is, of course, part of the poetic adventure.

Huachuma Archetypes

When the missionaries came to convert the millions of indigenous people in Peru, Huachuma got a new name: San Pedro. Since St. Peter is revered as the one who guards the gates of heaven, this is apropos. When I was on a master plant diet with Huachuma, however, he politely reminded me that Sir Peter wasn't known as the nicest fellow; stories of rampant misogyny and anger issues are prevalent, so Grandpa kindly asked me to emphasize his real name is Huachuma (sometimes spelled Wachuma). So, while Saint Peter is a namesake, he has much more relevant archetypes.

Because of his unbreakable bond to the energy of the sun, Huachuma also works with the archetypes of Apollo and Ra. The Greek god of the sun, Apollo was known for being the father of light, which is absolutely the energy of Grandfather Cactus. Huachuma illuminates what is hidden, giving us access to the awareness of our bodies and our planet in wholly expanded ways.

Apollo was also known as the god that brought disease and illness to the earth, which oddly enough, also has a parallel with Cactus. One of Huachuma's superpowers is that he highlights and amplifies physical discomfort, especially towards the last third of the journey (which can last up to 18 hours with a strong brew). He does this not to torture or harm his beloved grandkids, but to awaken us to what we might be ignoring. Our bodies don't just randomly contract illnesses one day, it's a gradual process, and Huachuma is utterly amazing at taking the whispers in our bodies and turning them into screams, if only for the evening, so that we are aware and motivated to take action for healing.

I had one amazing journey with him where, about eight hours in, I experienced the most paralyzingly painful sciatica surge. I ended up lying in bed with tears flowing in horrendous pain but grateful for the awareness that this had been brewing for a long time and my body had strong things to say. It was something I had been ignoring and Huachuma wasn't letting me hide any more.

In another ceremony I led with my medicine partner, a woman became quite ill with purging and tears. Huachuma isn't nearly as much a purgative as Mother Ayahuasca, so it's even more symbolic when cactus brings on a release. This beautiful soul vomited a vast majority of the day, and when I finally asked her what she was working with, she said simply, "Bulimia. I have been pretending it's not an issue, but it is, and

Huachuma won't let me hide anymore." This is the magic of cactus. He illuminates truths within and without. Apollo would be proud.

As would Ra, the Egyptian god of the sun. Ra is often cited as the creator of *everything* in Egyptian mythology, and the experience with Huachuma can often feel the same; he allows us to tap into our source energy and there's a distinct knowing that we, as humans, are completely made of God-stuff and therefore omnipotent in our manifestations. A journey with cactus is wholly unlike Ayahuasca and Iboga; while the ride can be 16+ hours in total, it's a slow opening into the full space of Huachuma and a slow ride back into our ordinary states of being. As the journey fully opens up, the ego gets smaller and smaller and smaller, until before you know it, you are fully in your heart and fully connected with all that is. These deep experiences with Grandfather are the closest moments to pure enlightenment that I have ever known. I don't just relate to Ra in these moments and hours, I am him. And all other deities that represent the purity and power of source.

Astrologically speaking, you can probably guess by now that Huachuma is all about the sun. He is most like Magic Mushrooms in that when we are completely enraptured in his energies, the most powerful way to fully express the fire and potency is by connecting to nature. As such, Huachuma ceremonies are most frequently held during the daytime and outdoors. The life force of every last living and inanimate object in nature is so undeniably felt, seen, and heard, we can often feel like communication with the consciousness of the planet is not only possible, but also palpable. Huachuma helps us bring back the fire of illumination into our lives; he is magnificent at reigniting passion and excitement for the missions we each carry. He also reminds us of the sacredness of consciousness; how blessed we are to know the power of breath and life force itself. Howard would call this the "holiest of holies"—something we experience every moment of our lives, but rarely in a fully conscious state. This is Huachuma's superpower, and a reflection of his divine partnership with the sun.

When to Work With Huachuma

I love this pulsing, incandescent plant so much, I'd rather ask when NOT to work with Huachuma. He's the kind of experience that, when deeply felt, we want the whole world to experience, because he gives us such a clear and empowering connection to love and peace, we recognize that is the energy that can heal absolutely anything.

San Pedro is used for many physical afflictions too, most notably alcoholism. I myself was able to step out of a years-long addiction to alcohol as a form of escape from my emotions with the help of Huachuma. He brings us back so palpably to our natural states of being, it becomes crystal clear how damaging and unsuccessful any form of escape really is. And a pure, potent dose of cactus welcomes us into the openhearted bliss that no serving of alcohol could ever match. The first time I worked with him, I realized this is the state of consciousness I had been seeking all along.

Huachuma is masterful at heightening our senses to the point where the mysteries of who we are and why we suffer can come into complete clarity. The shamans would use him to see and understand illness in their patients, and he therefore can help us do the same in our own bodies. When you're deep with cactus, there is no bad news—it's all sacred information. You are undeniably vibrating in the truth that consciousness never dies, so there is no space for fear of anything when Grandpa has you in his cosmic embrace.

I had a journey once with Howard that was particularly strong. We were riding in a rented van up to a magnificent spot in the Andes, and the medicine was coming on full force. We'd already had a flat tire on the journey and I was well aware we didn't have another spare should anything else go wrong. My mind started conjuring up fearful scenarios. What if we got another flat tire and were stranded in the middle of the Andes? What if the driver couldn't navigate the narrow, windy mountain road and drove us off the side (there were no guardrails!)? Every single scenario my mind threw at me only resulted in giggles. There was absolutely no possibility of anything that could actually scare me. Everything was all right. No matter what happened, I was safe. I couldn't stop laughing at this deeply felt realization. For the girl who felt anxious and in danger for the greater part of her adult life, this recognition of the truth of safety, at all times, was indescribably liberating.

Huachuma is heart medicine. He strengthens the heart and helps purify the blood. He can help heal depression and anxiety, and bring us back to the truth of who we are as sacred and protected beings. It is my sincere wish that everyone could know him in a deep and unbridled way at least once in their lives. If we all vibrated in the knowingness he awakens inside of us, there would be no racism, no misogyny, no hatred, no violence... just love. He is the golden chalice. The truth we all know but have forgotten.

Peyote: From the Earth to the Heart

Elements: Earth, Fire
Archetypes: Jesus, Wakan Tanka, the Blue Deer
Astrology: Venus

Peyote is a brother cactus to Huachuma; they both carry the primary alkaloid of mescaline and have extremely similar properties. The core differences, however, can be ascertained by the way they physically grow in nature. San Pedro reaches up to the skies, attempting to pierce the sun, and Peyote grows along the ground, barely peeking up through the soil. That tells us volumes about how the vibration of this heart medicine differs from its relatives.

Peyote is a medicine that is deeply felt inside the body. Purging is more common, as is the physical discomfort of the initial digestion. But, like Huachuma, this is heart medicine extraordinaire. Peyote has been a sacred medicine for tribes like the Huichol for thousands of years, and rituals still exist with this cactus, aiming to guide participants into a deeper state of love and connection with nature and themselves.

There is typically a strict structure around how the flow of a Peyote ceremony occurs; everything from the seating arrangements to the shape of the altar has deeply felt symbolism and meaning. Peyote is also normally an all-night affair, with rounds of medicine and food to honor spirit, and the centerpiece is often a soul fire that reflects the energy of the assembled group.

Peyote is wildly visual, insanely healing, and has thousands of years of sacredness. I know of folks who have literally healed lifetimes in their lineages of woundedness and pain, including one brave warrioress who took on the task to alchemize the Holocaust for her family, and it was a hell of a ride. But I am here to validate the efficacy of such work with plants like Peyote; they collapse the experience of time and space and allow us to reach back—or forward—and effect illumination, healing, and love.

Peyote Archetypes

The common symbol for Peyote is the blue deer: patient, extraordinarily aware, gentle, wise, and lightning fast. The medicine is potent, but there's always a gentleness with how he delivers his lessons.

Even when you're face down, purging in the dirt, the love is there. And like the deer, Grandfather Peyote sees all.

He also vibrates with the energy of what the Lakota calls "Wakan Tanka" or Great Spirit. Peyote has a purity and clarity that comes from source; just like Huachuma, he is medicine of the heart, so his messages come from a space of feeling, not thought. In that sense, he also holds a very Jesus-like illumination. Peyote is pure love, from the depths of the earth, with the energy and power of fire.

Yet the purity of Peyote in a spiritual sense has been affected by the attempted colonialization of the medicine in the 50s and 60s. Pharmaceutical companies like Merck were allowed to create pharmaceutical offerings from Peyote's main alkaloid, mescaline. It was, for a time, legal to have in this sense, but because the results of working with this substance were not repeatable with the scientific method—that is, western doctors couldn't predict what would happen when someone worked with mescaline or Peyote—the plant was eventually vilified. The same thing happened to Coca at this time as well.[31]

A few key Westerners saw the potential for the indigenous tribes who have revered and worked with Peyote for generations to lose full access to their sacred medicine, as the vilification of mescaline eventually led to the federal government making the plant completely illegal. Coca and Peyote are the only two sacred plants that are not even legal to have in their natural form, all because the pharmaceutical industry couldn't accurately predict how a plant spirit wanted to work with an individual being.

---

[31] *Mescaline, A Global History of the First Psychedelic.* Mike Jay. Yale University Press, https://mikejay.net/books/mescaline

This abuse and misunderstanding is carried by both plants, so if you choose to work with Peyote, please do so with the willingness to not only ask him for help in healing, but to offer him the same.

When to Work With Peyote

Peyote should only be experienced in the context of a sacred ceremony, from the people and tribes that have carried and protected this medicine from the beginning. If you manifest an opportunity to sit with an indigenous circle, it is a rare and special honor. Go if you have healing in your heart that you are seeking. Go if you have pain in your lineage that you feel the medicine can help to transmute. Go if you're ready to feel the connection to the earth in a way you never thought imaginable. Go to support the tribes that almost lost full access to their precious sacrament. But please go with reverence, knowing the history of the abuse white people have inflicted on this medicine and its traditions, with the willingness to not only ask for healing and clarity, but to give the same to Papa Peyote and his guardians. This happens through our humility and our willingness to support the indigenous tribes who have worked with and protected Peyote for thousands of years.

Magic Mushrooms: We Are Connected

Elements: Earth, Air
Archetypes: Loki, Merlin, Gnomes
Astrology: Uranus

In the shamanic tradition, we refer to the incredible collective of beings that comprise the spirits of Magic Mushrooms, otherwise known as *Los Niños*. They hold the distinction of being the only psychotropic plant we refer to in the plural; they are undeniably a colony of beings, a gaggle of mischievous, magical, interconnected mycelium with wildly sacred and powerful lessons. If you've partaken in a divine dose of Mushies, you've been through their psilocybin portal and you know how otherworldly, how both devious and delightful these creatures can be.

Los Niños are not plants, nor minerals or animals—they are fungi, which hold an entirely unique classification of life on this earth. They are part of the entire collective of mycelium, but Los Niños refer to those among them with psychedelic properties. All mushrooms play a pivotal role on our planet. But Los Niños, they are the ultimate teachers.

The main medicinal alkaloid in the Mushies is psilocybin, which holds loads of physical, mental, and emotional benefits. But to really understand how and why mushrooms are such potent healers and teachers, it helps to understand the role they play for the planet as a whole.

Mycelia are the bookends of life here; they alchemize dead animals and plants into new life. They get a bad rap in part because they are rightfully associated with death, but in the most divine, life-giving way. If not for these fascinating creatures, our Earth would be littered with decayed matter. Mushrooms allow the cycle of life to continue.

When we work with them as a sacred medicine, they allow the same thing to manifest within us. If you feel called to work with Los Niños, it's helpful to know what inside of you is dying or releasing, and what you would love to give birth to. They are bridge builders from the intangible to the tangible, and holding these clear and sacred intentions are most helpful in having a successful and heart-opening journey.

Additionally, studying the way mushrooms look and observing how they grow in the wild tells us scads about how they work as medicine. Mycelium is most prominent beneath the soil; mushrooms are the fruit of their labors, but not in the least bit the totality of their physical infrastructure. If you view the underground network of mycelium, it's hard not to notice that it looks strikingly similar to the network of the brain. Their systems of growth and connectedness are a direct mirror of the neurotransmitters of the mind; they form an underground connected grid of communication. And they don't just communicate among themselves. Trees and other plants use this network to pass information to each other; they signal when insects are attacking them, when disease has been developed, and when other crucial data are shared for survival.

In his must-see Ted Talk called *6 Ways Mushrooms Can Save the World*, mycelium expert Paul Stamets calls these incredible beings

"Earth's natural internet."[32] He eloquently describes the symbiotic relationship mushrooms have with almost all living things and the absolutely essential role they play in the harmonious flow of the planet. If you don't yet believe that we can't possibly exist without fungi, take a listen and get ready to bow to the mighty mushroom.

Mushrooms are like the old school phone system, both the infrastructure and the operator. They are master communicators, and they can do the same for our consciousness and for our bodies. When we work with Magic Mushrooms and have the addition of divine psilocybin, they create a portal of massive expansion and understanding.

Los Niños are profoundly healing for this reason. They can awaken in us the clarity we need to understand our traumas and dis-ease in wildly expansive ways. They can help us connect the dots of why we have certain destructive patterns and behaviors. They also help ignite the passing of information inside our complex physical and emotional systems that have potentially been dormant for years. Mushies help to bring light and illumination to our beingness, as well as deep healing, transformation, and rebirth.

As personalities, they are most notably the tricksters of the psychotropic world. They are mischievous and hilarious; another gift of their medicine is to remember to laugh at the absurdity of our wild and dynamic lives. It's a signature of a deep dive with them to, at some point, have uncontrollable giggles; they find the process of life and death and the consciousness we bring to both to be undoubtedly

---

[32] *6 Ways Mushrooms Can Save the World,* Paul Stamets, https://www.ted.com/talks/paul_stamets_6_ways_mushrooms_can_save_ the_world

delightful, and they invite us to celebrate it in the same manner. Niños embody the Shakespearean notion that "all the world's a stage," and they invite us to witness this with unbridled joy.

Los Niños Archetypes

Magic Mushies embody the energy of Loki, otherwise known as the god of mischief. This collective of healers has a definitive playful and devious side, always well-meaning but brimming with trickster energy. I once found myself deep on a mushroom journey with two sacred friends, insisting we put on scuba gear and take a shower. Which, of course, was obliged, as it was clearly a directive to let loose and be silly with the Niños. The most potent part of their medicine lies directly in the reminder that play is sacred, it is healing, and it is the essence of who we are.

They can be deceptive in their power, too. Los Niños are extremely potent psychedelic tools, but they reserve their full-blown omnipotence for the moments we typically least expect it. And they are aces at a sneak attack. When the medicine is crazy strong, the journeyer is thrust into a timeless portal full of a symphony of colors and sacred geometry and the brain becomes so lit up and electrified, you can be downloading the secrets of the universe at light speed. Depending on set and setting, this can either feel unspeakably empowering or devastatingly overwhelming. Mushies, like many other psychotropic plants, allow us to see the life force of all the Earth has to offer, and walls will breathe and dance as floors rise up to meet us and then scamper away. They can be extremely visual, and play all kinds of tricks with our feeble minds. While they are typically viewed as sweet and playful, if the portal is blasted open it can be one hell of a ride through consciousness.

Similar to the Loki archetype, Los Niños bring the magic, and therefore match the fabulous image of Merlin, too. Science has been fascinated with these creatures for decades, and more and more studies are coming out in recent times reflecting the magic of their healing powers. The Aztecs of Mexico are thought to have used Magic Mushrooms for physical healing and spiritual journeys, and tribes like the Mazatec of the Oaxaca region in Mexico still use them in sacred healing ceremonies. While they are not as well known for ceremonial use as a medicine like Ayahuasca, mushrooms have a very long history of guided journeys.

In a total feat of magic, Los Niños were even the cover darlings of Life Magazine in 1957, in a feature entitled *Seeking the Magic Mushroom*. The story chronicled the journey of R. Gordon Wasson, a mycologist who had traveled to Mexico to learn the indigenous history of the psychotropic mycelium.[33] Their magical qualities were admired and studied by science but this was eventually abandoned, mainly because Los Niños were not predictable with test subjects. Science appreciates repeatable scenarios and predictable outcomes, and these little devils defy the act of trying to pin down and repeat their patterns and behaviors. Just as Merlin's magic is not for mere mortals to recreate and understand, the magic of the Niños cannot be reduced to the scientific method. And so they were vilified and abandoned almost as fast as they were brought to the limelight.

The recent psychedelic renaissance, however, has brought psilocybin and its band of mischievous spirit guides back into the forefront of psychotropic studies. They hold the highest promise of infiltrating mass consciousness and assisting with the necessary healing. And so, they

---

[33] R. Gordon Wasson (1898–1986)

are back in the academic research space and getting their rightful respect and understanding. Merlin's magic created a disappearing act, but decades later, the magic is back. For the brave and loyal psychonauts, Magic Mushrooms never fell out of favor, but it's gratifying and thrilling to see them revered once more.

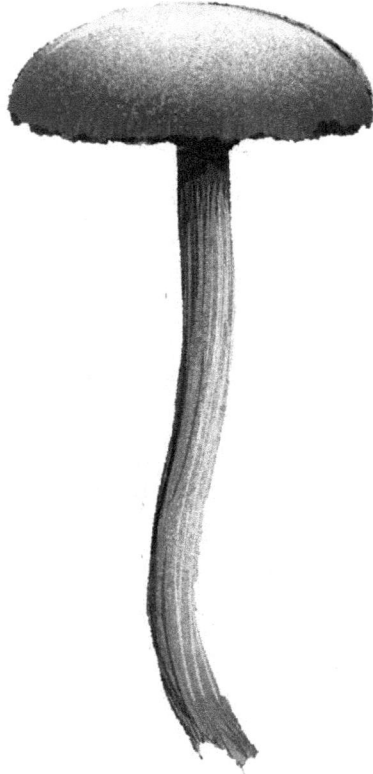

Astrologically speaking, Los Niños match the vibration of the planet Uranus. Ruler of the sign of Aquarius, Uranus is the quirky, cosmic, change-the-world planet that holds the energy of innovation and evolution. Uranus has zero patience for victimhood, and instead wants to celebrate even the most painful aspects of our consciousness, as it is the planet that wholly trusts intensity as a sign of growth, which is its only valid concern. Mushies are very much partners in this perspective. They giggle at our sob stories as a way to invite us into the same recognition; they, like Uranus, teach us that the painful events in our lives and in our consciousness are not the problem, the way we relate to them is. Los Niños and Uranus know the key to our salvation and liberation lies in acceptance and trust, not in resistance.

Uranus also encourages us to have the audacity to be an individual; to own our unique selves and to be unapologetic about that expression. Magic Mushrooms are wholly unique in the world of flora and fauna, and they absolutely love it. There is no timidness in their multidimensional wildness, their ability to embrace darkness and light, and even the sense of humor they exhibit around topics like death. Rather than coddle and appease us for feeling differently, they dare us to expand our limited views and lean into a bigger possibility of how to experience awareness.

Uranus is also the activator in our astrological charts, very much like a lightning bolt. Mushies can feel exactly the same for our minds; this energetic jolt of awakening that rewires neuro-relationships with past traumas and depression. They are electric, vibrant, intensely expansive beings who recycle lower energies into a higher state of consciousness. Just like the planet of electricity, they awaken new ways of being and help us blast out of old ruts and patterns.

When to Work With Magic Mushrooms

These quirky little beings are having a heyday, and they're just getting started. Once relegated to psychonauts looking for an altered and playful state, Psilocybin is now recognized by the psychedelic and scientific community as pure medicine. They are a fantastic alternative to anti-depressants and anti-anxiety medications, as they work to transform our minds on a physical and mental level. They have been instrumental for thousands of people to rewire the brain from an engrained fixation with past pains and depression, and can create new neural pathways that vibrate in much healthier ways, and connect to deeper states of joy and acceptance.

Out of all the psychotropic heroes, Mushies are the ones most likely to be selected for the experience of microdosing. Think of microdosing as a similar journey to taking supplements but on steroids, as working regularly with a medicine that can alter consciousness has way more potential effects than just your average vitamin. We will talk about microdosing more in depth later on in the book, but if you're one of the millions of folks taking daily medications to deal with depression and anxiety, Magic Mushrooms can hold the possibility of freedom from these drugs that often have a laundry list of painful side effects, and which don't even actually offer healing. Pharmaceutical drugs like these can be important bandaids during times of trauma and challenge, but they are by no means a path to healing. Psilocybin can offer that. Like their friend Uranus, this is revolutionary.

As a full-on experience, Los Niños are perfect for people looking to expand their world view. The core of their medicine lies in the authentic experience of connectivity to all life; they take things we may understand intellectually, like the idea that everything is connected, and allow these notions to be experiential. When you're on a full-blown dose of psilocybin, there is absolutely no denying that separation is a mental construct, not a reality. They can help us rediscover our place in the greater whole and connect us with the sacred sense inside that tells us unequivocally that everything is OK.

Like their friend Ayahuasca, Mushies are also fantastic if your mission is to understand death. The incredible role they play in nature reflects what they teach us in a spiritual sense. Mycelia are the alchemists of the living world; they break down dense matter such as fallen tree limbs and deceased animals, thereby creating new life. Without Mushies, our world would be a massive pile of rotting matter. Fungi are the creatures that take what has died and give it life again.

That's why a deep dive with Los Niños has the power to completely alter our perception of death. A five-gram feast is considered the "divine dose" that holds the highest possibility of granting the user a full-blown ego death. If you're lucky enough to experience this with Mushies, you'll come to know what death really is—a beautiful transition from the tangible to the intangible. These magical beings can blast open the portal of remembrance, taking us back into the cradle of the truth of who we are. Whether or not the experience is received as expansive or traumatic completely depends on set, setting, and our current relationship with our soul and ego. Regardless, it's one hell of a lesson about spiritual truth. Magic Mushrooms have the ability to rewire the brain and put us back into the center of our beings. They are one of the most important medicines of our modern times.

Ganja: Mistress of Darkness

Elements: Fire and Water
Archetypes: Mnemosyne, Kali, Shiva
Astrology: Chiron

No psychotropic plant is more misunderstood and abused than Ganja; also known as Marijuana and Cannabis (but for the love of all things holy, please do not call her "weed"). Ms. Ganja is an enigma. And she seems to like it that way.

It's a beautiful evolution to see Marijuana be more accepted in society, viewed as medicine and legalized in many cities and even states. But all this rapid growth and mainstream acceptance doesn't come without tangible repercussions. The very real challenges of working with Ganja are not what the naysayers and fear mongers espouse. But they're not non-existent, as the attached and even addicted among us claim. No, she's far more mysterious and powerful than what she gets accused of being—from either the pro or anti camps.

Ganja is called many things: healer, mistress, expander, angel, devil, and a gateway drug. Ask her if she identifies with any of these labels. She will likely say, "Why yes, I am."

To understand her superpowers, it's crucial to know how she works and how different she is from most of her contemporaries. She is not a ball of light; she works in the shadows. There's one very obvious way this becomes apparent: Unlike her sister Ayahuasca, Ganja can literally take our pain. Ayahuasca can show us what caused the blockage that triggers our agony and help us move it or change our relationship with it. Marijuana can go straight to the source and take it away in an instant.

That's how we know Ganja works in the underbelly. The space from which she dwells can reclaim our deepest aches, our darkness, our fears and resistance. But don't ever forget—the relief is temporary, and there are real repercussions if we use Ganja as a crutch.

Although the results of working with plants like Ayahuasca or Ganja can facilitate similar expansiveness and healing, the way they work with us to create these transformations are polar opposites. Plants often anchor their teachings through a space of light or darkness. Or both! Which simply means they work via illumination, or through the subconscious. Both are equally effective and sacred. We humans tend to enjoy one over the other, but healing is healing. However we increase our awareness and expand our consciousness is golden.

Light is simply illumination. Darkness represents that which is unconscious. We experience them in different ways, but neither space is better nor worse. They both hold profound teachings and lessons.

Marijuana works with us primarily from a space of unconsciousness (ours, not hers). This is why she is dicey. Working with anything that thrives in the shadows means it's very difficult to know when they are taking us on a ride.

Ganja oh-so-willingly takes us on that ride. She and Aya share that lack of apology. She doesn't care if it brings us into a full-scale life-centered breakdown. It's always for our own good.

Here's another reflection: A dark night on Ayahuasca can last the whole bloody evening, but in almost all cases, we feel reborn and amazing the next morning. That's the gift of moving consciously through our personal version of hell.

Marijuana can trigger a rough night too, but that's rarer. What she does is completely the opposite. If we are using her unconsciously to escape our lives—whether we know it or not—she will support that desire by slowly veiling our motivation, our drive, our life force. It can happen that over months or even years into the abuse we stop consciously showing up for our lives. We might start to retreat both internally and externally. And we will likely defend this position because... we are not aware. We are normally the last ones to realize when we become both addicted to being high and to hiding from our personal darkness by staying in the shadows of life.

Make no mistake, if you're using Ganja in a space of reverence and conscious intent, she has the capacity to heal through illumination too. Of course she does. But how many people do you know who uses Marijuana every time with reverence, respect, and sacredness?

If you're curious what it's like to work with Ganja in a ceremonial space and fashion, well then, I have a story to share. It's about that time Marijuana took me into her closet to show me who she really is.

For each of us, some plants are immediate love affairs, some are completely repulsive, and some take time and effort to connect with. It's obvious I've had a smitten union with Lady Ayahuasca since sip one—I've sat in hundreds and hundreds of ceremonies and apprenticed with several masters. She's tattooed all over my back and shoulders. I freaking love that girl.

MJ—that's been a much more complicated relationship.

Like most of us, I dabbled in high school and college. Unlike most of us, I hated being high. No matter the purity or the strain, no matter the potency or the cultivation, there has always been a malaise that I abhor when smoking Ganja. As an altered space connoisseur, I appreciate a substance with an edge and a serious boost. MJ makes me far too sleepy, checked out, and sometimes full-on comatose. I did and still do better with Sativa-heavy hybrids as I resonate with her mind-opening traits much more gracefully than the Indica body highs. Those are the ones that knocked me flat and challenged the already rocky relationship I had with my body. Yes, I'm aware, she's damn good medicine for me!

I didn't dislike her as a plant spirit at all. I just didn't like how she mixed with my chemistry. So I used her moderately all through my twenties. We were the girls at the party that would say hi and do small talk, but we never went deep.

Then I was in a long-term relationship with a wholly devoted Marijuana disciple. In the beginning, he smoked most evenings only. Eventually, he became a full on wake and baker. He smoked. All. The. Time. Especially when we were in heated arguments. I watched how he stuffed down emotions and hid from the truth of what we were manifesting by smoking.

Deep down, I knew that this was his choice. It's not Marijuana's fault. But I started hating that plant. She was an easy scapegoat for my misery.

During those days, I was all-in with my Ayahuasca work. It started becoming more and more apparent that the personal journeys between me and my mate were creating an irreparable divergence in the relationship.

One night, on the heels of a challenging discussion, he started smoking from the percolator nicknamed "Wernher von Braun" after the gentleman who created the V2 rockets, as it sent even the most

175

seasoned of smokers into bizarre, tripped-out spaces that landed them on our couch for hours at a time, recovering from the blast off as Cannabis Cosmonaut.

I had never smoked from this apparatus and I spontaneously decided it was time. My partner, of course, willingly (and very enthusiastically) obliged.

I centered myself into one clear intent: I wanted to know Marijuana. I figured if we got to know each other on a deeper level, I could let go of this anger.

Within five minutes, I was reeling. This was not a typical high. It was an onslaught. I excused myself and went to the bedroom, starting to freak out. The loss of control was manifesting. I knew this space so well from Aya, but I didn't expect it this evening, and I fought back. My partner followed me in and was an angel. He said all the right words. He reminded me that I knew what to do. I had to let go.

I went deep into a meditation, shortly thereafter, lying in the death position. MJ appeared to me clear as day. She looked more shadowy than human, but had a feminine outline draped in flowy fabric. She welcomed me into what she said was her home.

I started crying almost immediately. Basking in her pure and powerful energy was so humbling, so precious. She grabbed my hand and spoke to me.

"I know you know my sister. I know you like her better. But I will show you my magic the way any girl would—I will take you to my closet."

Closet? We're trying on clothes here? I followed in the vision and prepared myself to try on new outfits with this incredible plant spirit that was scaring and exciting me to pieces.

Her closet looked more like an endless subway station; a lonnngggggg corridor with cloaks hanging in a neat and orderly line as far as I could see.

"You know the 80/20 rule?" she asked me. "Ayahuasca is 80/20 in her favor. Twenty percent of your experience with her is your intent, the rest is up to her. She's bossy." I laughed out loud. Homegirl is HILARIOUS.

"With me, it's 80% you. Whatever people ask for, I usually give it to them. Only they aren't normally conscious of what they're asking for." We moved deeper into her closet.

"This section here," she pointed to a long row of cloaks, "these are for taking away pain. People ask for that all the time. I can do that. The pain shows up in other areas of their life, but I don't tell them that. They have to figure it out. I don't heal people because people have to heal themselves. If you define a healer accurately—that is, a person or being that supports someone in doing the work of healing—yes, I am that. But most of the time when people seek out a healer, they are hoping the healer will do the work for them. That's definitely not how I operate. Instead, I smother and cover and push down the energy. But it will show up elsewhere. It always does—unless they are doing the work to heal themselves."

She pointed to the right, and there were cloaks for as far as I could see. "Those are the usual. People lighting up to get high. Which means to escape their lives. I do that constantly. It starts off innocently enough. But months or years into this habit, shit starts happening. Not my fault. I'm just giving you what you ask for."

"See that cloak waaaaayyyyy down at the end?" I did. It was glowing and purple. "That's for the expansion of consciousness. People don't ask for that very often. It's my favorite cloak. I know how to go there, like Ayahuasca. But it's your fault for not asking."

I was buzzing and shaking and close to vomiting.

I could feel how intuitively she was connected to me, reading every heartbeat and every labored breath. She wasn't here to torture me. She was here to teach me.

"Thank you for visiting, Kat. It's not my fault. I give people what they're asking for. I'm a genie in a pipe. And we know those are tricky bastards. Also, you're welcome."

I felt such love for her; I could see clearly how she plays a sacred role for our society, which manifests as both the hero and the villain, depending on the lens. But she is neither. She is only a mirrored reflection of the energy we are swimming in.

It took me about an hour to come back into my body, but the experience was and is indelible. All the anger and rage I had for Ganja were replaced with reverence and gratitude. She is one hell of a plant spirit.

Ganja Archetypes

Because our lady of the shadows has significant spiritual roots in the Hindu tradition, she is often seen as divinely connected to Shiva the Destroyer and Kali, the Goddess of Burning It All Down. Ganja works with the energy of fire, and she burns away our unconscious barriers, our ignorance, and our disconnection from spirit. Marijuana is literally considered the most divine Prasad (offering) that Shiva can bestow on a recipient. Their connection is ancient, seen in various artworks and texts for thousands of years.[34] And because Kali is the one you call in when everything else has failed, Ganja holds much of that fire of decimation too. They are quite the trio of sacred destroyers.

Additionally, I love to connect Ganja with the lesser-known Greek goddess Mnemosyne.[35] Miss M has a tough name to remember, and ironically, she is the goddess of memory. She's most famous for being the mother of the muses, which is also an appropriate parallel to Ganja,

---

34 *The History of Cannabis in India*, Jann Gumbiner, PhD, https://www.psychologytoday.com/us/blog/the-teenage-mind/201106/history-cannabis-in-india
35 https://en.wikipedia.org/wiki/Mnemosyne

who can be so phenomenally powerful in helping us tap into our creative essences. But I find this to be a most poetic partnership when it comes to the topic of memory.

Since Ganja is infamous for shadowing short-term memories, the irony continues. This common accusation, however, is not necessarily supported by science—there is ample evidence that she is not the culprit we accuse her to be.[36] Regardless, this controversy warrants an exploration of the story that Mnemosyne represents.

The river Lethe is a sacred body of water that dead souls came to drink from, in order to wipe out their memories of their previous journeys. But if one had attained a certain level of conscious initiation, one could choose to drink from the dark waters of Mnemosyne's lake. Those blessed to sip from her mesmerizing waters had the good fortune to remember everything about who they really were. So, although the River Lethe's waters appeared much more clear and inviting, it's Mnemosyne's murky magic that held the key to memory.

Here's how this connects to Ganja: Those in mass consciousness who imbibe with her sans reverence and intention slowly lose their connection to memory. It's not punishment, but actually an expression of love. To lack reverence for her means to lack respect for oneself, and although we may not be consciously asking to escape and disconnect, we certainly are on a subconscious level. But if you work with Ganja in a ceremonial sense, taking her in with love and humility, she can ignite

----

[36] Acute and Non-acute Effects of Cannabis on Human Memory Function: A Critical Review of Neuroimaging Studies, G. Bossong, Matthijs; Jager, Gerry; Bhattacharyya, Sagnik; Allen, Paul, Current Pharmaceutical Design, Volume 20, Number 13, 2014, pp. 2114–2125(12), Bentham Science Publishers, https://www.ingentaconnect.com/content/ben/cpd/2014/00000020/0000 0013/art00005#Refs

the memory of truth in you, leading you to a deeper remembrance of the sacred connection of everything.

Ganja is like this with just about every reflection. Use her in habitual disrespect, and your life can crumble. Use her with the desire to partner and empower, with all the divine reverence you can muster... you and Ganja can create the life of your dreams. It's not the action, it's the intention. And she is the supreme teacher of this truth.

In an astrological sense, Ganja vibrates most with the energy of Chiron. I align these two because Chiron the comet is a force but often underestimated, and he represents the wounded healer. Ganja is a quintessential healer herself, but bears the wound of being highly misunderstood and disrespected. In Greek mythology, Chiron was a centaur, and highly regarded for his intelligence and penchant for justice. Cannabis is such an enigma in that she is stereotyped as creating a lack of intelligence in her habitual users, but that's only a reflection, once again, of their desire to check out. Converse with a reverent aficionado of her medicine and you are likely to find a highly intelligent, sharp, and creative being. Ganja is so brilliant; her mastership is hidden in plain sight.

Chiron was a master in the arts of medicine, herbs, music, and creativity, just like Lady Ganja. He was considered a gifted healer and a bona fide oracle, also in beautiful parallel with Marijuana. Chiron's complicated and rich mythological history ends in a tragic death whereby he isn't able to heal himself. Ganja feels like she matches this imagery; she is an omnipotent healer, a being that literally takes away our pain, and yet she often feels so heavy and wounded herself. I suspect that is a reflection of how we treat her as society, not her natural state of being. Even through the massive legalization efforts, she is still very much abused. Almost all legal Ganja is grown with pesticides and chemicals, and as the movement has grown, so too has the obsession with profits. She went from holding the stigma of "reefer madness" to now being used for egoic and pocketbook gratification.

Yet every single one of us that work with her out of love and appreciation do our part to create balance for her spirit. I know from experience that Ganja deeply desires to connect with us in joy; she wants us to recognize her, to go to her with conscious intention. If you're a fan of hers but you have not yet used your power of intention to chat her up, do so—you're going to be blown away with her intelligence, generosity, and sweet spirit.

When to Work With Ganja

The first camp of folks who gain great benefit from a relationship with Cannabis are those who experience severe anxiety and/or sleeplessness. Ganja has a natural ability to calm the nervous system and to create a beautiful state of sleepiness; especially the strains that are heavier with Indica. Sativa-heavy hybrids are better for mental clarity, creative connection, and the opening of the crown chakra. Indica is more connected to the body; thereby helping to calm us, bring us to deep sleep, and let us recharge.

As mentioned previously, Ganja also has the ability to eradicate pain. I suffer from bouts of severe sciatica from time to time, and Marijuana is the spirit I turn to for assistance in healing. When I'm in a full-blown attack, I go to her with vulnerable tears, and she cradles me and lessens the intensity of the pain. Indica Marijuana has also done more to help me heal my relationship with my body than any other medicine. She helps me feel beautifully connected to my body, and heals the desire to criticize and judge my frame. As a woman who has spent decades fighting against my beautiful vessel, I don't have enough words of gratitude to Ganja, my queen healer. She reminds me to love every inch of this home I dwell in, and there are few gifts more sacred.

People wanting a deeper connection with their muse also have beautiful success with Ganja. She can bring us into higher states of consciousness and help us tap into that elusive and magical creative flow. She works in our third dimensional realm, but she has access to the portals that allow us to travel to the cosmos; for creativity, for healing, for expansion.

Yet, unlike Aya and the ragtag multidimensional team, you gotta ask Ganja, or she will take you into the portal of numbness.

Ganja and Ayahuasca: Darkness and Light

A deep dive into the sacredness of Cannabis wouldn't be complete without addressing one of her biggest myths and accusations: Is she really a gateway drug?

Reefer madness was poised on the idea that not only was Marijuana a dangerous psychedelic herself, but that she opened the floodgates for many to become massive drug abusers. She's also been held as a ubiquitous partner to any other altered state of consciousness.

Those are both grave misunderstandings. Ganja is easily accessible and easily digestible, so she's a natural for first timers to choose when the curiosity of an altered state takes hold. But she is not responsible for the ensuing addictive behaviors, we are. And she most certainly does not go well as a partner to every other possible altered state.

Most prominent in the "we don't go well together" department is between Ganja and Ayahuasca. Mama Aya is the light worker. As much as she can take us through the darkness at times, those horrific nights on the medicine are trips through our individual and collective

183

consciousness; and as we all know, there are some dark, messy, ridiculously painful spots in there.

Ayahuasca is born from the underworld, but comes screaming up and out like a comet. She is a massive spotlight that illuminates the hidden things within us. Some of those suckers are nightmarish. It's not her darkness, she's just the friendly tour guide. And she knows that the more we face those demons and move through the energies, the more empowered, loving, and joyful we will be.

Ganja is different.

Ganja and Ayahuasca are both tremendously powerful teacher plants. One is used almost exclusively in this manner. One, let's face it, is not.

And it shows.

Ayahuasca gave me this wisdom once: Mixing two powerful plant spirits like her and MJ is a horrific idea in part because it's like trying to have an enlightened conversation with Buddha and Jesus at the same time. One in each ear, telling you the secrets of the universe.

And for all of you who think you'd love to have a chat with Buddha and Jesus, let's get down and dirty. Have you ever had a crazy super powerful spiritual conversation that was utterly, alchemically transforming and turning your world inside out? If you have, you know you could barely contain that wisdom. Do we really think we, as mere mortals, could handle two at the same time?

Buddha and Jesus, like Ayahuasca and Cannabis, have the same intention for mankind: Expansion. Awakening. Illumination. But each has their own way of working with us.

Here's a tangible example. Say you're working on an addiction to alcohol. Ayahuasca may swoop in and show you the core trauma that alcohol numbs, and she may encourage you to both feel that trauma and take a break from alcohol to see what happens.

Ganja often plays it differently, but with the same intent. She may encourage you to go deeper into your addiction, pushing a full on commitment to the act of escape so a breakdown can ensue. She knows a breakthrough can be facilitated this way, and so she sometimes works in partnership with the darkness, but still with our benefit held sacred to her intent.

If you sat with both plants and received both directives, the confusion is obvious. It dilutes the individual wisdom and creates a big ole cacophony, which can create stagnation or more repetitive patterns. Sure, there is no wrong answer no matter what, but we humans don't need to add more confusion into our spiritual paths. Most of us have plenty already.

People speak of Ganja and Ayahuasca as jealous plants; my experience is different. They aren't jealous, they just know what's best for us. Our dualistic minds can literally schism in the presence of just one pure plant spirit experience. Very few of us have the capacity to hold conscious space for two or more. (Emphasis on "conscious.")

So they demand we show reverence and sacrifice not because they like it that way, but because they know it's better for us in the end.

Yes, of course, I know many of you have had awesome experiences using Ganja in parallel with a gazillion other altered spaces. I challenge you to look hard at your life and find the places where the unconscious energies are manifesting. MJ especially is a tricky plant because she reflects our karma in spaces we often cannot see. So look for the cracks in your experience. Look for the spaces that feel stuck. Dark. Fearful. Heavy. Veiled.

If they aren't there, you can ignore me entirely.

Or don't look. Keep doing it your way, and that's OK too. MJ has all the patience in the world. She will show you the truth of how you're showing up over lifetimes if that's what you require. But make no mistake—she will show you. That's how much she loves us. When we respect her, we respect ourselves.

When in doubt, keep it simple when you're working with these powerhouse plants. One. At. A. Time. Be present and grateful that they choose to work with you, too. If you want the mysteries of the multiverse, they have them. But they will deliver them in painful and suffering-filled ways if you don't give them the attention and respect that such wisdom deserves.

This is the directive I have received repeatedly from both Ganja and Ayahuasca, and something I've discussed with gazillions of others on this path, including devoted followers of Ganja.

But it is not the final word. The final word about what each of us should do in any given moment when working with the plants lies with them, not us.

If you're working with any plant spirit, cultivate a deep connection, a space of listening, and trust them above all else. If they guide you to using more than one at a time, everything I say here is null and void. It takes a tremendous amount of self-awareness and integrity to know the difference between an egoic agenda and a plant-directive missive, but regardless, our results are always there to point us to the truth if we can't see it any other way.

Ganja, Ayahuasca, Chacruna, Huachuma—they're the bosses. We are just the vessels of experience.

Bufo and Vilca: Back to Source

Elements: Air, Water
Archetypes: God/Source/Creator Energy
Astrology: Neptune

Bufo is a mysterious and all-powerful toad whose secretion is used for one of the most profoundly mystical and out of body experiences available. He is 5MeO-DMT-based, a substance famous for ego deaths, interdimensional travel, and sending people completely and totally back into the space of unity and/or nothingness.

Vilca is a plant-based 5MeO experience; an entirely different spirit and personality, but with the same vibration and lens of sending people back to source.

These substances are not for anyone who is unstable or shaky with their egoic and tangible world relationship. They are also the most important experiences to enlist the assistance of an extremely well-trained and well-meaning guide who is an expert at creating a safe container and can keep participants calm and protected the entire time. Although the journeys only last twenty minutes or so, lifetimes occur during them. Many people meet extraterrestrials or interdimensional beings; even the most skeptical among us. The exit and reentry moments are by far the most precarious; they will show us how we relate to the absolute, and back to our egoic selves. Some folks are graceful and surrendered, some encounter existential fear so paralyzing they might need months or years to recover. These are no-joke substances. And as such, they are utterly magical.

The 5MeO trip reflects to us our relationship with consciousness outside of the attachment to ego. That's typically a very complex relationship to confront, both on the level of our soul and ego. Each of them may have entirely different ways to relate and react. But if you are called to working with either of these beautiful spirits, you are absolutely a courageous student of consciousness. A full dose of either Bufo or Vilca is truly a transformative experience. I am not even able to write much about either as it's so out-of-body—and therefore, out-of-mind—that words just can never do these journeys an iota of justice. These are the big guns, and are to be treated with the utmost caution and respect.

Bufo and Vilca Archetypes

The only remotely appropriate archetype for an experience so catapulted out of duality is source itself; the representation of unity, of ego-less existence. This is a journey to understand creation and our roles in that dynamic. It's a chance to explode out of the holographic subject-object perspective and consciously (or not) experience oneness. As such, the only archetype that makes sense is God herself.

Astrologically speaking, Neptune is the perfect reflection. This placement in our charts shows how we relate to the intangible world; Neptune rules dreams, altered spaces, and anything soulful or out of body. He indicates how we relate to the nondual world, the space of non-linear thought, and our relationship to spirit itself. Those with sensitive or conflict-filled Neptune placements in their charts would be wise to proceed with caution when deciding to work with Bufo or Vilca.

When to Work With Bufo or Vilca

5MeO is the mother of all altered spaces, so turn to this experience if you're ready to know the truth about consciousness. It's imperative that individuals who work with these medicines have a very well-trained and capable guide, and that you also have a firm foundation of stability and trust in yourself and the universe as a whole; if someone has a belief that the world is here to punish them, not welcome them back to truth, Bufo can be devastatingly difficult to integrate. While it's an experience that lasts only 20 minutes or so, it can be one you integrate for many years after. It's akin to a death experience; an unforgettable yet impossible to understand or describe catapult out of ordinary consciousness and into the arms of the infinite. Proceed with caution, but proceed with curiosity and joy too.

Honorable Mentions:

There are multiple plants that don't quite fit the typical entheogen category but deserve endless accolades. These are two that I simply cannot leave out.

Tobacco

Elements: Earth and Fire
Archetypes: Sitting Bull, Father Earth
Astrology: Earth

So misunderstood, yet so powerful. Vilified as a cancer creator, yet possessing supreme healing powers. Tobacco is quite possibly the most misunderstood and abused plant spirit in existence. And yet he still loves humanity so, so much.

Almost every known shamanic tradition incorporates sacred tobacco in one way or another. I call him Father Earth, as he shared with me once that he is literally unified with the consciousness of this planet, as her masculine counterpart, full of divine protection and unconditional love.

Tobacco's superpowers start with his immense ability to help us humans feel grounded and embodied. Mapacho, as he is called in the

Amazonian jungle, is a sublime protector and a messenger of the spirit world that helps carry communications to and from this realm to those that lie beyond. He is an amazing partner in sacred ceremonies and master plant diets, helping to clarify the visions and messages received from the spirits of the plants.

Yes, he is addictive, but that's precisely why he's sacred; he forces us to be in complete integrity with the reasons why we choose to work with him. In the traditions I practice, we actually work with tobacco in multiple forms. We love smoking Mapacho in ceremony, creating a bubble of protection and a warm energetic hug for anyone who needs it. We imbibe our heartfelt intentions into the smoke and then blow it into an individual or a space for blessings.

We also work with Rapeh or Hapé, a shamanic snuff made from tobacco ash and Tsunu that is administered up the nose and is absolutely a heavenly vibration. Since tobacco has the natural ability to lower blood pressure, Rapeh is a fantastic medicine to use before a journey with entheogens, as he helps calm anxious nerves and relax the body and mind.

Ambil is another common form of tobacco; this refers to a thick paste that is rubbed on the gums to bring activation of the masculine.

Finally, we sometimes drink a potent tobacco tea as a way to deeply connect with this spirit; this is the most risky way to consume tobacco, as it can cause intense purging, sweating, and disorientation, but it's also immensely empowering and brings a deep sense of internal connectedness and peace. Because tobacco can be dangerous to consume, it's essential to work with him in this way only via a trained practitioner, but a Mapacho Master Plant dieta is a powerhouse experience.

Coca

Elements: Fire
Archetypes: Hermes, The Muses
Astrology: Mercury

Another vastly misunderstood, magnificent plant spirit, Coca, is a very important and sacred member of the entheogen club. Coca, also known as Mambé in the Colombian tradition, is the ultra-feminine angelic spirit that is known as the ultimate truth serum. The locals believe that when you have a scoop of powdered Coca in your mouth, you cannot tell a lie.

Coca can be taken as a tea—maté de Coca (Coca tea) is a very popular drink along the Andes, as she's amazing at curbing the effects of altitude sickness. Coca is superfood to the max—she's loaded with high-density nutrients and plant-based proteins. She is most commonly used as a powder; her leaves are dried and pulverized into a very fine ash-like consistency. Additionally, she is often paired with Ambil, the tobacco paste. He brings the masculine component; she is the feminine. Her psychotropic superpowers are centered around vitality; she is an amazing source of energy, clarity, and life force.

Yes, Coca is the same plant that cocaine is derived from. Cocaine is an extracted and chemically altered alkaloid, and it's essentially the energy of the plant being raped. She is nothing like that atrociously dark energy; Coca is generous, playful, and exceedingly kind. But we have abused her fiercely, and sometimes she asks us to clean that vibration in her too. Yet when you work with her in her pure form, the lift of energy is there, but the comedown is not. She, like Peyote, is completely illegal to have in her raw form; it's a wild travesty, because she is even more gentle than caffeine, sweetly giving us a boost of energy and truth. It's a damn shame that she is seen as an evil plant—this couldn't be farther from reality. She's an absolute angel and I hope there's an awakening around her healing abilities and specialness soon too.

But What About the Synthetic Medicines? Are They Sacred Too?

LSD, MDMA, DMT, Ketamine, synthetic Psilocybin; these, too, are rightfully labeled medicines, but they lack one major component that those discussed above possess: Organic consciousness. Everything that is born from the earth, be it crystals or plants or humans and animals, all have an organic consciousness that cannot ever be reproduced in a lab. No matter how much science advances, even with AI, it will never recreate organic awareness. Only the earth can do that.

That does not mean they don't hold an important place in our healing and awakening. I have personally had profound and magical experiences on LSD and MDMA in particular. But I no longer reach for any of these substances, as my personal choice is to work with what nature creates for us. That feels like the natural way to me. But I would never deny anyone the right and opportunity to seek healing in any way that calls to them. The myriad of ways to alter our consciousness exists for a reason, and anything can be healing if we treat it as such.

But as discussed in the differences between DMT and Ayahuasca, choosing to fly the cosmic spaceship without a consciousness guiding the journey is undoubtedly precarious. It requires great reverence and skill to ensure the safety of the trip and the efficacy of the healing. This is not impossible, but it is often overlooked by either the clinical or recreational settings these substances are typically used within.

I can no longer go to music festivals and concerts where people are passed out, suffering, and/or completely oblivious to the darkness they are attracting. It hurts too much to witness, partly because I have been that person many times before and it's taken a lot of healing with the plants to come back to my connected center. That said, we learn in all ways.

Therefore, I will not outline the archetypes and gifts/challenges of all the synthetics, because it is not my role to openly advocate their usage. This is not the path I have chosen. I support those that do with integrity and respect; I am not the one to speak to the safe ways to work with them as it is not my focus. So this is an acknowledgment that they do exist, they belong, but it's ethically a slippery slope to bypass nature and rely on what is man-made. I personally trust Mama Earth to provide the healing I need, not a chemist. This is just a personal choice. I support yours.

Testimony #4: Rebecca Keating

Shamanic Practitioner, Founder/Owner of The Shaman Sisters

I was working as a Registered Nurse when I first began my journey with sacred plant medicines. I had already been on the Shamanic path for several years and was called to Grandmother Aya. Prior to going to Peru, I had watched every documentary and read every article online about Aya. I always tell people, it was nothing like what I expected and can never really be explained in words—it was such a profound, life-changing experience.

Plant medicines have expanded my consciousness and greatly impacted every area of my life. They connected me to my purpose of being of service and doing what I love—starting my own business and my shamanic healing practice. Working with the medicines Aya, Kambo, San Pedro, and Psylocibin have allowed me to release deep seated fears, wounds, and traumas. They have helped to show me my unconscious patterns and how to bring myself into deeper alignment.

I have seen others completely transform with plant medicines, from healing addictions to becoming more loving, forgiving and patient. We will all get what we need to be our Highest Selves.

Rebecca Keating
www.shamansisters.com

Mystery #7: Fasten Your Seatbelts: Essential Elements to Enjoying the Cosmic Journey

Creating a Safe and Sacred Container

When working with entheogens, you get what you give, in all respects. The major difference between a recreational romp with a substance like Psilocybin and a ceremonial journey all comes down to set and setting. This is what shamans and guides have known for centuries. If you do the work with ritual and intention to create sacredness and reverence, a portal of love and healing can open. Dive in without paying careful attention to all the elements of your environment, and the energies contained within, and chaos can ensue.

You know that feeling you get when you walk into a holy place, like an old Catholic church or a ninth century Buddhist temple? Even for those of us who have zero connection to the faith or belief systems, you can feel the holiness, the magic of a space that has held sacred ceremonies of any kind. Spaces hold energy. They are imprints of everything that has happened in their walls. Our ignorance or lack of ritual does not protect us if we are opening up the doors into other realms and states of consciousness. This is why creating a safe container to do this work is absolutely essential to a favorable outcome.

Ask and It Is Given: The Power of Intention

Consider intentions as the tools that help create a safe container within our own consciousnesses. They are also the tent poles that help the mind have a place to hold on to if it feels like your brain gets tossed into a blender (a common sensation on charismatic psychedelics).

Intentions lay the foundation for the communication with the plant spirit and are the basis for measuring success and forward movement after the experience is over.

There is a good deal of neuroscience on "free will" and determinism, but if we observe our own experience, we can see that while we may not have the cartoon version of freedom our egos imagine that we do, we certainly have the capacity for intent and consent. Consent to having that intent!

The art of setting intentions is wholly rooted in emotions, not words. It's helpful for our minds to have a clear sense of what we're working on, but it's not necessary to the plants. We overthink intentions because we have big ole brains that desperately want to participate in experiences that literally blow them to bits. Having a clear intention or two before going into a journey does two core things for the mind:

1) Intentions give our minds something to hold on to if and when shit gets real. When we feel the loss of control, it's helpful to remind ourselves, "I'm here because I want to heal!" "I'm here because I want to release trauma!" etc. They are like tent poles that tether us back into the present moment and help us say yes to the experience.

2) Intentions also allow us to measure what really occurred as we integrate the journeys. Going into an altered space with only a bit of curiosity can mean that we have nothing to measure the success of the experience as we reflect on it. Asking for information about something in our lives gives context to an already confusing adventure, and that's so vastly important as we make sense of what happened.

There's no such thing as a bad intention, but there are more powerful ways to reflect on them. For example, if someone is working with fear, I like to guide them away from an intention like, "Take me into my fear," and instead express it as, "Help me handle my fear more gracefully." We will learn what is necessary with both requests, but asking ourselves to focus on the positive—in this case, being less fearful rather than in the fear itself—makes for a higher possibility of grace before, during, and after the ceremony.

But as I said before, words are really just there for us. What the medicines work with is our inner truth, which is accessed through our emotions. When people come to ceremony in a flood of tears and desperation, I love to remind them there's no greater truth to bring to the altar. A broken heart is an honest heart, and it allows an opening that lets the plants right in. As Leonard Cohen said, "There's a crack in everything / That's how the light gets in."[37]

Microdosing vs. Divine Doses: Can Less Be More?

Microdosing medicines like Psilocybin has started to become a fashionable trend, and for very good reason; the entheogens, when worked with reverently and safely, can help to rewire the brain, balance neurotransmitters, move through trauma, and physically plus emotionally help to create a new foundation to work from. The protocol for microdosing each entheogen is very personal to what the individual is working with and the potency of the medicine they have access to, but it typically involves taking a small dose of the medicine every two to three days. Ideally, the individual will also have a larger dose every few months or so, but that is not required.

Unlike pharmaceutical pills, it's extremely difficult to create a "one size fits all" protocol for entheogenic use. A person's emotional state, physical issues, and sensitivity all play an important role in determining dosage and frequency, as does the existing relationship to the plant. This is not pill popping, it's a connection that is built upon. So microdosing requires an entirely new mindset that the Western medical world doesn't yet know to espouse.

What's the secret to success microdosing? In essence, it's doing the opposite of what the Western world has taught us. Most of us take supplements and pharmaceutical drugs in a wholly unconscious way.

---

[37] *Anthem*, The Essential Leonard Cohen, Leonard Cohen, https://www.youtube.com/watch?v=bN7Hn357M6I

We pop a pill, down it with water, and go about our lives, rarely giving these substances a second thought.

For any mergence with plant medicine to be effective, however, we have to bring our awareness and intention to the mix. Working with plants in any fashion is, at its foundation, a relationship. Imagine if you treated your friends in the same way... no dialogue, no deep listening, no reverence. It wouldn't be much of a relationship. Treat microdosing the same way.

Whatever medicine you choose to work with, in whatever manner, deserves your full attention. Every time you decide to ingest, smell, or otherwise merge with a plant medicine, take the time first to make a connection. Tell the plant what you are seeking. Let them feel your vulnerability around the things you aim to heal. Ask them to reveal more of who they are. And then take the time to listen.

It helps to bring your awareness to the parts of your body that you seek healing for as well. Visualize your body receiving and merging with the plant medicine as you take it. Bring light and movement and joy into your beingness. Treat the whole, beautiful process with respect and excitement. We get what we give, after all.

This simple yet limitless commitment to focus and intention can be the one factor that catapults your success with the plants. If you want them to give their all to you, give that to them first. That's the formula for co-creating magic.

Thou Shalt Not Trip Alone: Why an Experienced Guide Can Make or Break Your Journey

Ayahuasca and her tribe of plant friends are wildly potent psychotropic substances. They can catapult any brave soul who gobbles down their tea into a tirade of terror so intensely convincing, death can feel like a blessing. There are a bazillion tales of massive breakdowns caused by entheogens on the web, and yet many are choosing to make their own brew and drink medicines like Aya all by their lonesome.

Is this a good idea? Should anyone ever work with something like Ayahuasca alone?

If you're a Westerner reading these words and contemplating this option, the answer is a resounding, blazingly loud NO. As in, absolutely positively no, no, no.

But there are exceptions. (Aren't there always?)

Let me explain.

Psychotropic plants like Huachuma and Magic Mushrooms can take someone unexpectedly into a painful, emotional process, and without a trained sitter, the participant could exit the experience with more trauma, not less. Precisely the opposite of what we are aiming for. It's not common for these substances to invoke that level of fear and deep psyche work; yet it happens. It most definitely happens. If you're someone who puts safety first, you'll want a guide that knows how to navigate the darkest corners of the mind. Even better, you'll have the wisdom and reverence to work with these plants only in a ceremonial setting, with someone who knows how to create a safe, loving container, and who can drive the spaceship back down to earth safely.

Ayahuasca, however; she's the Mother of All Medicines. And she will school you something fierce if you go to her without the deepest respect for her power.

Many who are called to drink Aya have already jumped down the rabbit hole many times. Aya is the ultimate consciousness expander, so it makes sense that many folks who find their way to the medicine have already journeyed with things like Ganja, San Pedro, mushrooms, LSD, etc.

Even if you're an old pro at navigating these spaces, you are not trained to handle the true depths of Ayahuasca.

Aya is like other altered spaces in that she brings light to the unconscious and has the capacity to take us on that delicious cosmic ride. There can be brilliantly colorful visions, incredibly expansive experiences, and awesome access to the secrets of the universe.

Her differences, however, need to be respected, or the results could be traumatic.

Ayahuasca is the medicine of duality. So, although she takes us out into the cosmos, she also takes us deep, deep within ourselves. She is the ultimate teacher of, "as within, so without."

This is where the chaos can kick in. The dark nights of the soul Ayahuasca can induce involve bringing our demons to light. Some of us surrender into that blessing, but most of us fight like hell, at least in the beginning.

Resistance creates suffering. Suffering creates a desire to escape. And an ego that wants to escape a psychedelic has just entered a full-on Chinese finger trap.

Try to fight with Ayahuasca, and you will lose. In this case, losing means potentially freaking out. Even if you've never been brought to your knees by another psychedelic, Mother Aya can take you there.

If you need to be humbled, and most of us do, Ayahuasca will gladly take on the task. She will show you no mercy (which is actually a reflection of her love). And if you're by yourself when this occurs, there's no limit to what might happen in that space of total panic.

- Would you ever contemplate doing your own dental work?
- How about teaching yourself to skydive?
- Would you ever perform surgery on yourself?

Choosing to do Ayahuasca without a trained shaman is just as ill-advised as taking on all of the above.

A trained Ayahuasquero has spent no less than 7-12 years with a Maestro learning the intangible lessons of this mysterious energetic process. They have already faced the darkness within themselves hundreds of times. While they may not be fearless, they have developed a deeply intimate relationship with the medicine that is anchored in unconditional trust. They have dieted multiple master plants and seen every conceivable breakdown in the medicine space. They are not afraid of the darkness, and the ways in which people resist it.

They also know how to handle psychotic breaks. They know how to handle a room full of intense purging and waves of traumatic release.

A great shaman is a guide into the beautiful unknown. They are confident and compassionate. And well equipped to handle any egoic meltdown.

Drinking Ayahuasca without the presence of an expert means that you're on your own if and when the shit hits the fan. There is absolutely no possible way you are immune to a meltdown, regardless of how many trips you have successfully navigated. And there is no possible way you can know how wildly intense this can be. How vulnerable you could become. How dangerous you could be to yourself if the medicine were to take you into the depths of your unconscious fears.

If you drink alone, you likely leave yourself completely open to all the energies you are messing with. It smacks of disrespect. It reeks of ego, this notion that you can really handle anything that comes your way without years and years of training.

Messing with energies is not a joke. Taking a medicine that is a portal into all that remains unknown in your psyche should never be taken lightly.

Whether you hold that demons and devils are real or you believe it's all just in our minds is actually irrelevant. The perception of danger equals danger. If you think you're in trouble, you are. Fear feeds on itself. So whether you externalize that experience or believe it's all coming from within matters not. Darkness is, and when it hits you, there is no limit to how humbling that can be. This is what a shaman protects you from, the demons on the outside and the demons within. They are one and the same.

If you've never experienced anything energetically that you felt you needed protection from, your turn to be humbled could be in the next dose you drink. You don't know what you don't know. Talk to anyone who has drank enough Ayahuasca, and they will have tales of the darkness. They will have those shocking moments when it was finally their turn to beg for help.

It took me nine years, but when I finally hit that place of terror, I literally had to ask someone to make sure I didn't drink Drano, or do anything to hurt myself. The energies were so unbelievably intense, my ego was willing to do anything to escape. The shaman poured himself into helping me move through this darkness, and I wept in gratitude.

Had I been alone, I might not be here to write these words. That's no exaggeration.

Almost everything the shaman does for the circle involves protection. They call in the helper spirits and plants to guide us in our journeys. They sing powerful icaros to help move energies, heal our hearts, bring on the purge, and guide us into every conceivable emotional experience.

They hold that space with strength and love, so that we can all feel safe enough to go inside ourselves and do the work.

When you work alone, you are acting as the guide, the protector, and the participant. That's just too many hats for most.

So if all of this is true, why don't we hear about all the nightmarish experiences from individual drinkers? They are out there, but not in droves. If I'm right about the dangers, how is this explained?

In the infinite wisdom of the medicine, it's very, very common that those who work alone have milder experiences.

The reasons why are gorgeously complex.

First of all, shamans train for years to make a brew that is truly powerful. This is not a matter of ordering the right plants on the internet and reading an Erowid thread for the recipe.[38] In this sense, our ignorance often saves us. It's not easy to make a potent brew. Nor is it in any way intuitive to know how to integrate our own energies with the tea or to understand the esoteric ways a shaman imbibes it with love and protection. Would a beginner chef know how to masterfully create a dish of beef wellington? A fluffy souffle? It's the same with a potent, balanced, love-filled plant brew; this takes time, practice, and oodles of finesse.

---

[38] https://erowid.org/chemicals/ayahuasca/ayahuasca.shtml

Likewise, when we do anything alone, on some level we know the inherent risks. Whether we're conscious of it or not, this creates a deeper sense of caution, and it inhibits our ability to totally let go.

Going it alone means we miss out on the magic of learning from someone who has been blazing a trail. It's like studying a craft with a professional vs. trying to learn by reading an online thread in a forum. The real magic happens when we're vulnerable, inspired by those who came before us, and learning by example in a space of safety.

When you drink alone, resistance to the depths of plant medicines can often result in a lighter experience. That's another thing they gift us when we work alone; they often keep things a bit more on the surface.

Yet that can be dangerously misleading. If your intention is entangled in any way with a disrespect of her potency and/or a grandiose view of your abilities to navigate the darkest of energies, eventually, you're going to learn your lesson. How that manifests is a mystery. Trusting that it will happen is not.

We also don't hear a lot of singular horror stories because people are sometimes too shamed or humbled to publicly share. Admitting that we were wrong, that we were arrogant, or that we were complacent to the power of a sacred plant is no easy task.

Quite often, these humbling experiences show up outside of ceremony, too. We may not see the correlation of our world falling apart to any disrespect for energies we have unconsciously toyed with. But it is absolutely all connected.

Just because we don't see the truth of these entanglements doesn't make them any less real.

Now, here's the flipside. There are a few sacred reasons to drink Ayahuasca all by yourself.

The obvious is if you are training with a master, and he/she has told you it's time.

I was in training for almost 6 years before I started solo work. And I did so under the guidance of my teacher. He always knew when I was embarking on a solo experience. He met me there in that space to guide me. I played his icaros on my iPad to keep his presence strong. I asked the medicine to be gentle at first, so I could find my own foundation and confidence with her in a solo setting.

It was a long, purposeful, uber-respectful process.

And it absolutely changed my life, and my relationship with her, in beautiful and connected ways.

You might also be a devout and experienced sitter, not necessarily called to facilitating, but desiring a deeper connection to the medicine. If the shaman you sit with agrees it's a good idea and is willing to supply you medicine that you trust is pure, this is an enormous blessing.

Finally, please note all these cautions and concerns are directed to a primarily Western audience. I'm not picking on the Western world, but I am noting that the vast majority of us are very disconnected from spirit, and thus very connected to our minds. It's this attachment to mind and ego that creates a potential schism in ceremony. It's like asking someone who is very unfit to suddenly run a marathon; they are going to need a lot of training. And many of us are exceptionally spiritually unfit.

So, if you've grown up in an indigenous culture or at least connected to one, and you've been around spirit most of your life, these warnings probably do not apply. I am aware of many folks in Brazil and Peru that do solo work, but they receive their medicine from local shamans, and they are simply expanding their bond with an aspect of their cultural upbringing. That is a beautiful thing.

If you're renegade and grandiose enough to consider a solo journey, none of this may have landed yet. You may think you're immune to the downfalls. You may think I'm crazy and dramatic and that my fifteen years of experience with this process doesn't supersede what you know about your ability to get altered and handle yourself.

Well then, I can't stop you.

I just ask you to deeply consider your motivations for moving forward.

Intention is everything with this process (and with life in general).

Keep yours deeply rooted in respect for the medicine, and this lineage. Keep yourself as humble and open as you possibly can.

I'm not looking to scare anyone; I am only providing you with more information. I want everyone to have a glorious experience with this life-changing medicine. That requires awareness, reverence, and a lot of personal integrity.

Choosing the Right Guide: Ensuring Your Safety

Sitting in a plant medicine ceremony requires a tremendous amount of trust. You're going to be crazy vulnerable. You might get to purge in a bucket with complete strangers in a space you've never visited before. You're likely to hear songs in a language you've never heard of. You might see wildly intense visuals, have a profoundly new relationship with spirit, expand your conscious awareness into darkness and light, and have all manner of cosmic journeys.

Please don't do any of this without fully vetting out who you're sitting with.

When I organized for a gazillion years, I was always disturbed by those who came to the initial interview with no questions or curiosities. You literally need to trust your physical, emotional, mental, and spiritual safety to the crew you are sitting with. Folks often assumed I was interviewing them, which was partially true—but what I really wanted was for them to interview me right back. The more they asked me questions, the more I knew they were ready and serious about the task at hand. This also gave them the opportunity to feel my love and transparency, which always created a deeper space of safety. And in this work, the feeling of safety is absolutely everything.

Every circle you have the chance to sit with should have one or more organizers accessible for an initial consultation. They should make you feel completely cozy, have a high degree of transparency, and give off the energy that your comfort and education are of the utmost importance.

If you're looking to sit with a group that doesn't do any or all of this, please don't sit with them. If they don't have the time, care, desire, or knowledge to make you a priority at this stage, you cannot trust that they will have your back if and when the shit hits the fan in ceremony. You cannot trust that they can hold space if multiple people need assistance. You cannot trust much at all, and that is the most important aspect of this work.

I absolutely don't mean to scare anyone, but I must also be honest with you—medicines like Ayahuasca and Huachuma can create a full on dark night of the soul. They can feel like your worst nightmares made real. You can reach a place where death feels like a gift. A place where you think you couldn't handle another millisecond. That you'll combust if more energy or darkness or fear or whatever-the-hell-it-is comes through you.

And if you need help, if you need a calming force that is skilled in moving you from hell to heaven, I truly hope you've found a circle that knows how to step up. That's their job, after all. That's why you're paying to participate, following a strict protocol, and trusting a very unfamiliar process. To be protected. To feel safe enough to go deep, face your demons, and do this glorious and sacred work.

Below is a list of all the questions I myself would ask any organizer about the process. Don't take this as an exhaustive list, however, as you may have more of your own. These are the essentials—make sure you have clear and solid answers about each one. Don't feel like you're an annoyance for asking all of this; you have every right to understand the process.

If anything doesn't feel right, trust that unequivocally. This is not a place to take chances.

Here is my core list of questions to ask any plant medicine group or facilitator–I call this the *Essential Plant Medicine Pre-Flight Q&A*:

1. How long has the organizer been working with the shaman or practitioner?

2. How did she or he come to know the medicine? How did she or he come to know the healer(s)?

3. How many attendants are there? How many sitters?

4. Is there any doctrine or dogma that the practitioners hold sacred? (For example, some ceremonies are facilitated by the Santo Daime, which has a religious element. Those ceremonies

are very different from the others, so this is crucial to be aware of.[39])

5. How much does each ceremony cost? Are there discounts for multiple nights? What is included?

6. What is the ceremony space like? Is it a home or business? What's the parking situation? How many bathrooms are there? How much space does each participant have? What should/can you bring? Water bottles? Blankets? Pillows? Tissues? Yoga mats? Crystals?

7. What are the advised preparations? What foods should be avoided? What can participants eat? Is it OK to smoke Marijuana before ceremony? Is sexual activity beforehand okay, or should it be abstained? Any other recommended prep? (Every circle is different with this protocol.)

8. What health conditions are prohibited? What medications cannot be mixed with the medicines? Make sure to have full disclosure on any health issues and the medications you are taking. *This is crazy important.*

9. What time do people gather? What time can people leave? Can you sleep in the ceremony space or are there other options? (Don't trust any circles that let you leave right after ceremony. There should be a safe place for you to come back into your body for as long as you need.)

---

[39] Santo Daime Church, http://www.santodaime.org/site-antigo/doctrine/whatis.htm

10. What is the shaman's training? Who did he or she apprentice with, and for how long? What lineage do they practice? Is there anything modern or personalized about how they lead the ceremonies? What other healing modalities has the shaman studied? Is there a chance to connect with the shaman before or after ceremony?

11. How does the group handle someone who is having a difficult time? What do they recommend a participant do if they are personally struggling? Any advice for riding the wave?

12. Is talking allowed? Dancing? Can participants sing or play musical instruments? Are there rules around movement or going to the bathroom, etc.?

13. Is the use of tobacco or smoke used during ceremony? Can participants smoke (either in the circle or at a designated outdoor area)?

14. What other plants or medicines are used during ceremony?

15. Where does the medicine come from? What's in it, exactly? Who makes it? What connection does the shaman have to those who make the brew? Is there more than one kind of brew for the group? If so, how is it determined who gets what? (If they don't know the exact particulars of the medicine they are working with, this is a big red flag.)

16. Do the shaman and attendants drink the brew?

17. What is the ceremony process? What time do people drink? Is it one by one or all at once? Do people come up to an altar or are they served in their space? Can participants drink more than once if needed? How many rounds are offered? Is there

doctoring? If so, does everyone receive this assistance? Does it happen at a central altar, or in the participant's physical space?

18. Are buckets provided for purging, or do participants bring their own? Are they responsible for cleaning them after ceremony? Is it OK or encouraged to dump out used buckets right after purge, or should people wait till after ceremony?

19. What is the referral process for interested friends and family?

20. How do they honor discretion? Do they ever advertise on Facebook or Meetup or public places? (Don't laugh. Some circles do and it's appalling. Unless you're in a legal setting.)

21. What happens at the end of ceremony? How do people know it's over? Will there be fruit or snacks served? Is water or tea available? Is it OK to talk after ceremony? Does the shaman leave right away? Will someone be around in case there are people struggling?

22. Is there any aftercare or assistance with integration provided? What if someone struggles in the aftermath—can anyone assist and offer guidance? If so, what is their training or experience?

23. What do they recommend in the aftermath? Should the diet be continued? If so, how long? What about sexual activity? Watching dark media? Drinking alcohol or using Marijuana or other drugs?

I hope this helps you find your perfect circle to sit with! It's wild how many are popping up all over the world. If you are called to this work, the plants will find you. So, trust that if you feel the desire to sit coming from the depths of your soul, the opportunity is manifesting—or has already.

The goal here is simple: Make sure you get to do this work in a safe and loving space so that it facilitates healing, not more trauma.

Why So Many Shamans Abuse Their Power

In all these years of taking part in Ayahuasca and Huachuma ceremonies, I've seen a gazillion miracles. Bodies healed. Traumas purged and untangled. Massive awakenings and consciousness expansion. A hell of a lot of joy and bliss and gratitude.

But I've also seen unbelievable darkness. Shamans who intentionally manipulate people out of anger and a hunger for power. Ones who lack integrity and think it's appropriate to doctor people when they themselves are in complete breakdown.

And the sexual passes during ceremony. Oh yes, that happens. I've been there firsthand. Twice. The pain, betrayal, and sadness are more than I could ever express. (So are the lessons, by the way, so I have zero regrets. I accept perfection in all.)

This has led me to, very consciously, explore why so many shamans go dark. I have heard many, many accounts from people who have had challenging, confusing, and straight-out traumatic experiences. Part of that is our filter, I get that. Some of us are so lost in our stories of trauma, we project them on everyone we meet.

But there are some seriously rogue "healers" out there, and this deserves to be called out.

Here's the first big issue: The expectations we put on the role of shaman are nearly impossible to meet.

To any of you who have the aspiration to achieve this sacred moniker, bless you to pieces. If you're just starting out, you have the gleam, the glow, that burning desire to be of service and to partner with these glorious energies. I had it in spades. I also had the "Can a white girl from Montana really do this?"

No one can tell you how hard it will be. Egos don't believe it anyway. We hear the sordid tales and think—I can handle it. This is my destiny. And that's true if it IS your destiny. Either way, it doesn't matter. Whether you feel called to sit or to serve, it's your journey. The destination matters not.

But why is it so bloody difficult to do this job?

Because it's not a job. It's a goddamn lifestyle. It's a balls-out full-on commitment that is all-consuming and will ask ALL of you. More, actually.

This process becomes your wife, your husband, your mother and father, your first-born child, your best friend. You must be willing to sacrifice anything and everything to do it, because trust me, that will eventually come due. And if you're not willing, it's going to kick your ass. Which it will do anyway, but it's easier when you're a willing participant.

So, what ends up happening isn't rocket science—eventually, no matter how disciplined a shaman is, the world creeps in. The dark, nefarious, temptation-filled, deliciously deviant world. And if you tangle in duality and think you've got the upper hand... oh, my friend, you have lessons to learn.

Part of the reason a shaman gets too big for their britches lies squarely on the shoulders of the participants. Especially us Westerners. In many traditional tribal cultures, the medicine man or woman is just another member of the community. What they offer is cherished and sacred, but no more so than anyone else. Every task is essential to survival, so there is no hierarchy.

We Westerners have a different perspective. All this energy stuff is magic to us, and we get awed by what we perceive the shaman can do. But the pedestals we put them on guarantee they will eventually fall off. It's irresponsible to see them as anything but human. It's not fair to expect perfection. If we appreciate the job that they do without elevating their ego, we can also help them not get so inflated that the universe must orchestrate a downfall.

So, it's up to all of us to strike a balance. Give someone your power, and you are asking them to abuse it.

Anyone in any position of authority has an ego to wrestle with. And that right there is a full-time job. But what happens to people in leadership? They can get lazy. They think they've reached the top. They think they have nothing left to learn.

And that's when the energies take over. We are here to live and learn, after all. Not to arrive and get all snooty.

So, to own this role of healer means you have to be in wild integrity with yourself and your core tribe. No BS. No hiding anything. You have to own your shit. Own when you're triggered. Own when you're afraid. Own when you're sexually attracted to someone in the circle. Own when you want to get drunk and run away.

At the very least, you own this to yourself and the medicine. You have elders that can keep you honest and aligned. You work with the medicine all the time with humility and a sincere desire to see your delusion and heal your hurts.

And yet, you can't let your guard down in ceremony, as you are the gatekeeper, the protector, the tone setter.

Don't ever, ever work with a shaman who doesn't work tirelessly outside of ceremony on his or her own path. How that appears is personal. But if you get the feeling they have the perspective that they've "arrived," I would simply arrive somewhere outside of their circle. Because that's poppycock.

So it's a full-time lifestyle. And just when you think you've got it down, spirit will throw another curveball to teach you another lesson.

A shaman often lives on the outside of the tribal community for a reason. Isolation helps to keep things clean. The more they tangle with the stories of the people they serve, the more it can compromise their ability to keep us safe inside the ceremony container. *(I know this one well. I do not exaggerate when I say this was almost a deadly downfall for me. Let's just say aloofness is not my superhero power, and an abundance of attachments and entanglements almost did me in as a shamanic practitioner.)*

In that, self-care is also essential. We've all heard the adage "Physician, heal thyself." This is never, ever a past tense statement. It's always in the present. And that happens with self-care. A LOT of self-care. Every day, without fail. Eating right, meditating, time with nature, connection with guides, hot baths, loving relationships, etc., etc., etc.

We gotta love on ourselves to have the love we put on others be authentic. And healing is nothing but love.

At the end of the day, anyone who wants to be a healer has to be damn clear what their true intentions are.

I'm going to go out on a limb and suggest that most people—whether they admit it or not—are attracted to power.

Money is power, so it's deeply entangled. And most of us have a very dysfunctional relationship with the spirit of money.

But, put the awesome power of the plant spirits in the hands of a power-hungry ego, and dear God, craziness can ensue. If they are adept at turning around whatever happens on you using spiritual rhetoric, that's a dangerous dude (or dudette) right there.

So, shamans go dark because this is duality, and that is its core job—to bring us our lessons of expansions through trials and tribulations.

Ideally, said shaman who has a dip into their own humanness takes a break. They have the awareness to not project this on others. They own it to the people that love them and have the power to ask for help. But that doesn't always happen in such a sweet and tidy way.

Quoting his teacher from whom he would finally break away, Carl Jung called the energetic bond that happens between someone in a healer role and the recipient "transference." He emphasized that whatever is deeply felt within the practitioner will be passed on. If a shaman is in their own darkness and not in integrity with it, they still can't hide the truth from a cracked open client. Especially in an altered space.

What you're looking for as a participant is not perfection. It's not a guru or an uber-human. It's just one who is authentic. They have a clear method of working on themselves. They exude compassion, but with healthy boundaries. They have a love of integrity and know that's the key to success.

Trust me, even those shamans that really seem to fit the part of guru, that have thousands of adoring subjects and allow themselves the pedestals doled out by so many... they are very, very susceptible. The taller the pedestal, the harder they will fall.

And they better love and respect this medicine more than life itself. If you don't feel that, run.

Since most of us don't get access to the shaman before we actually sit, ask the organizer all of the key questions I've shared throughout this book. Don't just blindly trust, especially if your instincts are triggered. If you don't have access to the answers you need, then it isn't a safe circle.

It's disturbing to me how few people ask these questions when they sit with a new circle. Knowing you're in good hands is literally the most important part of this process.

And because this is a wild world and our egos are extraordinarily complex, it's up to us as participants to take responsibility for where we sit and who we do this work with. Thankfully, we have lots of options these days, and there are people doing this with love, integrity, and pure intent.

Just because there are a lot of bad seeds doesn't mean there aren't plenty of golden threads. And just because even shamans are human doesn't mean they can't adeptly dance with their darkness and keep others safe in the process. Safety, however, always rests in our own personal hands. We keep ourselves safe, first and foremost, and we do that through instinctual curiosity. Paranoia isn't necessary or even very helpful, but discernment is.

Finally, a last unexpected note on safety. Some of the Western-led big-name retreats purport to create safety by having allopathic doctors and nurses on staff. I get how tempting this is to trust; we are conditioned to believe the Western medicine world is superior. I'm here to report otherwise. It makes the ceremony space more dangerous, not the other way around.

When you sit with trained facilitators, you are, in a sense, already in a hospital. These people are highly trained to know how to keep you safe, in all ways. Western doctors are rarely, if ever at all, versed in the nuances of working with plant medicines and energy. So, what happens is this: You go to sit in a ceremony with doctors at the ready. Let's say you're a diabetic who is afraid of having a diabetic reaction (high or low blood sugar). The medicine might push you to believe you're having an episode, and you start to ponder if you really are getting ill. You request for a doctor to come verify your worst fears; that your blood sugar has skyrocketed. Said doctor arrives with much distraction and fanfare— I've watched this firsthand—they come racing into the sacred space with flashlights and medical gear. As soon as they enter, the entire circle is now encased in fear. This fear is contagious after all and can turn a beautiful journey into a nightmare.

In all the times I watched a doctor come on the scene during my tenure at this big-name retreat, not once was the medical emergency real. They would report that all was well, race out just as fast as they raced in, and we, the facilitators, were left with a colossal mess.

Yes, it's lovely to know a hospital is within a reasonable driving distance for the very rare occasion it's needed. But don't be fooled into thinking the Western perspective trumps the indigenous way of healing. If you've hacked off a limb, the allopathic way is genius. If you're experiencing the symptoms of fear that could potentially lead to a physical ailment, that choice could actually add to the trauma, not heal it.

If you feel called to sit with plant medicines, trust your guides, not someone who has zero training in the complex world of plant medicine. Respect the traditions you are entering into; please don't feel it is necessary to bring your own. In other words, leave your allopathic doctor at home. When you are in an authentic ceremony setting, you're already in a hospital; albeit a type that might be new to you.

Mystery #8: Creating Protection and Dancing Through the Darkness

I reference protection and safety probably no less than 1.2 gazillion times through this book, but what does that actually mean? And what do we need protection from?

When I started this journey, I was the quintessential naive and overly optimistic apprentice. I didn't just have rose-colored glasses, I had stainless steel lenses I thought were opaque and were actually blinding. I didn't really buy into the idea that safety was needed; I was a tried-

and-true non-dualist with the whole "it's all love" story down pat. I firmly believed that if I didn't put any emphasis on the idea of evil, it wouldn't manifest.

Sweet, I was. But I couldn't have been more ignorant.

I, like so many of us, learned the hard way. I had zero discernment, was insta-trusting, and dove into any opportunity to journey with any and all medicines in any and all scenarios with any and all practitioners. As a result, boy howdy do I have some *stories*.

What kind of stories? Nightmarish ones. Trusting my safety to someone who started making highly inappropriate sexual passes to women *who were under the influence of Ayahuasca* (he went to jail for it long after we parted ways). Sitting with a famous Westerner who intentionally puts other uber-potent psychotropic plants in his brew and literally laughs at the chaos, offering zero support for folks who spin out. Entangling with a leader still in the throes of active addiction (which I didn't know about, but felt the danger and ignored it), resulting in the most horrifically dark ceremonies of my life.

What we don't know can, in fact, hurt us deeply. And while I still hold that on the highest level absolutely everything comes from love, I am no longer in denial that the vulnerable parts of all of us don't receive everything as love. Not here in duality. And since what we perceive is in fact our reality, it is now my absolute obsession to always be mindful of safety and protection whenever I do this work for myself or others. Without that awareness, the lessons we learn are so much more painful and difficult.

To all those who hold the same perspective I once did, that all this black magic and darkness talk is just fear-based poppycock, the stuff that Carlos Castaneda books are made of and nothing more, I give you one challenge: Have cyanide for dinner and let me know how that works out.[40]

Assuming you did not take that challenge and are indeed still here, you must then agree that there are things that are inherently dangerous about life, energies, people, and consciousness itself. While we can learn through dismissed discernment and naivete, I invite us all to listen to a deeper wisdom: Our intuitions.

This is a ubiquitous topic that all of the plant medicines, in varying degrees, highlight for us: The ways in which we betray ourselves, our intuition, and our boundaries. Who are we if we deny the truth that lives within? Why do all this incredible work of healing and self-discovery if we only ignore the deeper wisdoms that spring forth?

One of the most important words I have learned to say with increasing confidence and self-love is No. No thank you, not yet, not in a million years, etc. Ayahuasca likes to say to me, "Where there's smoke, there's fire, love—listen to the whispers of the smoke so you can avoid the intense lessons of the fire." I have so often dismissed the importance of my own safety and intuition that I have been utterly annihilated in the fire I could smell from a million miles away.

So let's listen to that wise inner voice when they let us know something is not aligned. We work so hard to access that intelligence inside us. Quite often, what that voice is asking for is this: Protect yourself. There's no need to realize our instincts were right all along by getting burned.

Protection then—what is it, and how do we create it? It's a state of consciousness. A mindset, a way of being. When we feel safe and secure,

---

[40] Carlos Castenada, https://www.castaneda.com

we are. When we feel frightened and vulnerable, we are that too. Most of us white-knuckle our way through the terror, but the core of shamanic training shows us that we can be successfully accountable for creating the safety we deserve.

First, though, we must fully define what it means to be safe. This isn't the kind of safety the ego craves. We would love to walk in the world knowing we'll never get hurt, we'll never die, and we'll never have the rug yanked out from under our happy little feet. Duality doesn't offer such promises, however, except in delusional spaces. So, we must extend our wisdom beyond the realm of duality to find a bigger truth.

To feel safe, we must learn to trust life—and death. We must embark on the existential mission to experience our consciousness outside of the limitations of the mind. This is where plant medicines are mind-blowingly special. They alter our consciousness to the point where we realize, without question, that we exist as aware beings without the confines of a mind or a body. Once we start to crack this code on a large scale, real safety starts to spring forth.

The only thing that dies is resistance. We are, truly, eternal. So, while it's a dangerous and contrasting world here in duality, and pain is oh-so-real, we are ultimately safe in that we cannot be destroyed. This is a big, beautiful video game; made to feel intensely real, but the cosmic joke is this—death does not exist. Transition does. Transformation, yes. But endings are only rooted in fear, not reality.

This is all good and well to mentally ponder, and many of us trust this intellectually, but not yet embody. Our beautiful vessels have a consciousness too, one an old teacher of mine called the "body mind." That primal vibration has existed since the beginning of time for one reason only: Survival. This is why even the most awakened among us will fight tooth and nail to avoid perceived destruction. The body and mind are mortal, and as such, they will do just about anything to continue existing in their current states. No amount of intelligence can circumvent that primal urge at times. Instead, we can turn to powerful practices of safety and protection.

I divide the art of protection into a few core categories. There is no handbook on how to do this for ourselves, as we all resonate differently with various modalities and techniques, which also shift throughout our lives. What works for me today might not tomorrow, so diversifying our toolkits with lots of protective methods is extremely important. If you don't already have a practice of creating peace and safety for your inner self, try it on for size; it's a game changer even for folks who don't experience daily anxiety. For those that do, this is non-negotiable.

Category #1 is Plants. Look on the altar of any medicine man or woman, and you'll see a myriad of plants used to create a cocoon of safety. Common ones include Sage, my primary go-to—she's a fiercely fiery plant spirit that creates deeply felt boundaries with zero apology. She can purify a physical space, our bodies, or our energies by clearing out clutter and negativity, and wrapping us in a smoky cloud of magical protection. Palo Santo is a divine wood used for smudging that is also tremendously soothing. Drinking Lavender calms the nervous system and allows us to feel grounded and safe. Tobacco—or Mapacho if he's jungle-sourced—is often a plant many shamans would never ceremony without. He's massively protective and calming, and we use him in multiple forms as a result. Mugwort, Juniper, Fir, Marosa, Rose—the list of plants offering mortals the chance to learn this energetic art form is varied and potent. Whichever is calling to you, go there and create a solid partnership. If we're going to do the work of leaving our bodies and traveling the cosmos, we are wiser to do so with safety and care. And with a bundle of badass partners.

Category #2 is Crystals. If you're a tactile being, clutching a piece of the earth that vibrates with love and safety is irreplaceable. I'm a big fan of Obsidian; a sacred stone to the Egyptians, among many others. Black Onyx is an amazing protective crystal. Rose Quartz, Tourmaline, and even Amethyst can be used for creating an impenetrable bubble. Remember, if we are fully connected with our sovereignty and are grounded in the self-loving principle that no one and nothing is allowed in our field, it is a universal truth. But we can't have our fingers crossed behind our backs. That's where our protection partners keep us honest. If any of these crystals help you feel immaculately cared for and guarded, then make them your BFF and bask in that truth.

Category #3 is Visualizations and Meditations. After I pour the first cup of medicine in any plant ceremony, I spend a good chunk of time visualizing protective armor over every inch of my body. I spin blue cocoons around my frame, infusing it with pink sparkles and vibrations that make me feel completely secure. Then I extend an energy grid of rock-solid protection through the entire space I'm working in, paying extra attention to doors and windows, the portals through which energies enter. Once the space feels strong and protected from all sides, including top and bottom, I put protective bubbles around every participant. By the end of this ritual, it's very clearly articulated from my heart to the medicine and the entire space that only love is welcome, and I will not tolerate the interference of energies that wish to teach us through suffering. Most importantly, I allow the most vulnerable parts of myself to feel completely nurtured, which means I can convey that same sense of "everything's OK" to everyone in the space. I can't create safety for anyone I'm working with if I don't already feel it myself. This is my way of keeping myself honest.

For some, it's poetry, chanting, and the shine on a cosmic mirror. Whatever works for you, keep flexing that muscle. Don't wait until you feel compromised and panicked to find what works; be proactive in finding your preferred method of safety, and then when it's needed, it's already an intuitive connection.

Navigating a Dark Night of the Soul

If the plant medicines have taught me anything, it's that fear born from resistance is a beacon of light that can guide one to a massive breakthrough. In other words, the darkness is an angel in disguise. Oh-so-easy to declare, oh-so-difficult to embody. But let's try.

Before I dive downnnn into all things hellish, let me first add a qualifier: Substances like Ayahuasca are limitless, magical medicines that do not take us to hell; rather, they show us how we define things as hellish and give us the opportunity to change our perspective to expand into a more universal definition of love.

Sometimes they do this by providing a gorgeous and beautiful trip to happy land. They know how to be subtle and heart opening and playful. Ayahuasca in particular has a sense of humor that is off the charts. She has shown me so much love, so much gentleness, so much tender, motherly nurturing, it's hard to even begin to describe it.

Part of her expression of love, however, is finding the blockages we hold in our psyche that cling to the story of fear and darkness. She does not heal those places; she blasts them open. Sometimes that feels amazing and healing and restorative.

Sometimes it feels like a journey so outrageously, mind-blowingly terrifying, it makes our worst nightmare feel like cuddling a puppy.

The medicines teach us this: Hell does not exist. It's just a state of mind.

What is hell, really? A place full of fiery brimstone and devils that requires an extra dose of courage and antiperspirant?

Not exactly. What we define as hell is deeply personal. It changes and shifts as we transform in our lives too. Hell is whatever we fear and resist. Whatever we haven't expanded into and understood. And that's different for all of us. Aldous Huxley's *Heaven and Hell* articulates this distinction beautifully.[41] He wrote that heaven and hell are actually two contrary portals into mystical experiences. Yes, the flavor of each is oh-so-dramatically different. But each portal leads to the same destination: Awakening. It doesn't matter how we learn. We all are coming to know the same truths, whichever path we take up the mountain.

In the context of Ayahuasca, some people fear the onslaught of demonic visuals. I've seen snakes eating disemboweled babies, been chewed on by a horrifying alien, watched all manner of dark sexual images writhing behind my eyes—and grinned my way through it. I've watched enough *Faces of Death* type films in my goth days that imagery alone can't phase me. That is not hell to me. It's just a dog and pony show. But to others, it's just straight up devil-driven.

Some find the purge hellish. I was never one of them. Maybe because I'm a recovered bulimic, the idea of vomiting out my toxic impurities has always been a blessing; an easy and welcomed release, even when my insides were turning inside out. I still have the internal cheerleader voice saying thank you and yes please, help me let this go!

Emotions are another stickler. Revisiting past traumas, sitting in a pool of rage or sadness, these are very un-fun moments. I've helped many folks navigate this space, and many would definitely call them hell. I

---

[41] Aldous Huxley, *Heaven & Hell*,
https://www.fadedpage.com/showbook.php?pid=20171022

understand that. But my definition is different. Less tangible. Hard to talk about without going into fits of shaking.

The First Trip to Hell Is the Easiest

Ayahuasca loves me. I know this because she wasted no time taking me to the underworld.

It was ceremony number two that started the dark-side journey. I knew it before I even drank that night. Despite the fact that the first ceremony was absolutely gorgeous and gentle and insanely beautiful, I could feel the energies on night two. I was absolutely terrified. But I wanted to know what this was...

That ceremony, and many others in the near future, would prove to be intensely difficult dark nights of the soul.

Each time they unfolded, I thought and espoused, *that was the worst night of my life.*

And the best. Because the lessons were priceless. Always so on target. Always so transformative. And so, I was willing to risk another wild ride in order to learn the secrets of the universe.

Every time, of course, I figured, *it can't get worse than that.*

Every time, of course, I was wrong.

There was a night someone asked me this innocent question before ceremony:

"Kat, does it ever get easier?" I laughed and said, "Yes! You get the hang of it after a while."

Ever have those moments where something you said earlier in the day comes back to haunt you in ceremony?

Yes, that.

Every single night I sit with the medicine, I have an intention. That night, I asked her to show me more of who she is. Show me the parts of consciousness I hadn't yet explored.

And to help me completely surrender.

This night, I was spinning before I even drank the medicine. Thirty minutes in, I wasn't in this universe anymore—I was in a centrifuge of terror. Everything had spun into overdrive. I couldn't see straight—my eyes were trembling, making everything look like it was attacking me. My body shook like it was plugged into a power plant. I became the thunder.

I emerged into the darkest of energies. The space where hatred is born. Where fear takes root. She showed me the energy of murder and rape. The force that causes all chaos, insanity, and violence.

Death would have been a gift in those hours. I was certain this was too much for me.

I'm normally a rock in ceremony, but that night, I could barely hold on. I moved manically at times, trying to find a space that was comfortable. At least manageable. Something to lessen this horrible, wretched, awful, terrifying state.

Nothing helped. This was my version of hell. It came, she told me, because I asked about surrender. I asked about that which I did not know.

When my teacher brought me up to doctor me through direct singing of the icaros, he knew I was in trouble. He handled a lot of the most precarious situations we navigated with humor, so he leaned in and said: "Kitty kat, you asked for this. Don't forget to breathe. It is just energy."

Just energy. Yes. Just. Energy.

That didn't help at all. The doctoring made it worse too. More energy to push me into the vortex of awfulness. I WANTED OUT.

Hours later, I was still in the grip of insanity. Internally, I begged for mercy. I was channeling William S. Burroughs, who, like poet Allen Ginsberg, drank ayahuasca in the 1950s, and declared, "All I want is out of here!"[42] I tried to hide my tears so that the circle didn't feel vulnerable because the attendant was losing her shit. It was obvious I was in my personal hell; however, for the first time in nine years, I was That Girl. To say it was humbling is like saying donuts taste OK. Understatement. There are no words.

And in the thick of it, I had the clarity. I knew what was happening.

This, too, was love.

Yes, I was face first into the molecular madness of death and destruction. I felt completely out of control because when you surrender, there is nothing left to hold on to. All attachments fall away. And the abyss feels so vast and dangerous and frightening.

But there was some other essence there, some other truth.

---

[42] William S. Burroughs, Allen Ginsberg. *The Yage Letters.* https://www.amazon.com/Yage-Letters-William-S-Burroughs/dp/0872860043/

I turned to all my tools and guides for help. Agua de Florida. Sage. Lavender. All the amazing plants that supported me in tangible and intangible ways. As I let them in, I felt that space of OK-ness.

The madness didn't lift, but something else entered. Something else gave me contrast and clarity.

That something was a force of love so strong and undeniable, I knew it had to be from the center of the center of the center of the All. This was God-love. Source sparks. The essence of Prana.

This was life force.

And even in that space, my mind kept looking for an escape. Minds don't fit in there. It's the proverbial eye of the needle—straight out of the Bible, Matthew 19:24. They can't control it. Can't contain it. So it literally feels like you've gone past the edge of crazy.

Maybe I could drink Drano to make this better. Maybe I could go running through the streets screaming for help. These were very, very real desires.

Or maybe I could just let it be. Love it to pieces. Say yes to this madness. Trust that it was indeed all love. Recognize that this unattached, free-fall into the abyss was actually heaven once I got used to it... once I trusted that there wasn't anything here that could harm me.

Let go. Surrender. For real this time. Not with my fingers crossed behind my back. That was the challenge.

I managed to fall into the energies with my whole heart that night, just as the shaman was singing the closing icaro. Bhakti cannonball. It was the one and only night he sang the closing song to me.

Hell became heaven.

Strike that. I realized there is no hell.

Hell is only the dark side of heaven. Nirvana is Samsara (Nagarjuna). Each is an aspect of the One That Is.

In fact, heaven doesn't exist.

Everything Just Is.

Either we embrace that as truth, and walk in trust and love, or we fight and beg for something to hold on to.

The things we hold on to are attachments.

Attachments cause suffering.

So, to un-suffer, we let go into pure terror. And if we're really, really, really lucky, we realize it's just the fear of the unknown.

That we are and always were OK. In fact, we Always Are!

That we are loved beyond words.

That we are love. And nothing but.

I know there's an endless number of ways to reach this place. With all my heart, I thank Ayahuasca for being the tour guide. The most horrific night of torture turned out to be the most genuine act of love I will ever know.

Here's the rub: The deeper we get to know the energies of bliss and joy, and the more adept we become at creating our own safety, the more the darkness has to amplify in order to take us to our edges. There is no space where we are suddenly masters of these intensities. They are limitless in their strength. The finite meets the infinite. So, the journey necessitates that we learn to accept this is a part of working with plant medicines, and a part of consciousness. Either we learn to walk through hell with a smile on our faces, or we stay tethered to the horrible vibration of resistance.

Now, let's discover some ways to support ourselves when the devil invites us to tea.

Creating Allies to Combat the Trance of Fear

Because we learn such wisdoms not by reading someone else's account of making friends with darkness, but by experiencing it ourselves, allow me to offer a myriad of tools and modalities in which anyone can navigate a dark night of the soul—sourced by plant medicines or life. Dark nights don't discriminate. And by the way, they can last a lifetime, as the soul doesn't care about time, but instead, just wants to grow. It takes what it takes. So, arm yourself with as many tools to work with the darkness as you are able to cultivate.

First and foremost, as clichéd as it may sound, create a conscious connection with the magical power of your breath. This is the steering wheel for any anxious experience. It's one of the body's only functions that is both controlled by the subconscious, and when we choose, our conscious minds. Scientist John Lilly was fascinated by dolphins, as each breath they take is conscious. We, too, can slow down and speed up the breath at will. We can intentionally pull it deep inside our vessels, sucking in life force, grounding into our bodies, and breathing out toxicity and stress. But we have to do so *intentionally*. There's a reason every spiritual practice has an emphasis on conscious breathing; it can literally take us from pure panic into a serene state of presence and bliss. But we can't wait to connect to our breath when hell breaks loose; daily practice is the key. Whether this is through meditation, breathwork, yoga and other movement, or a simple commitment to focused attention, learning to consciously breathe is a game changer when the curveballs of life—and altered spaces—come swooping in. And swoop in they shall!

Here's another "out there" but extremely effective tip: Get to know your spirit tribe. In shamanism, we are very serious about befriending our animal and plant totems, our guardians and spirit tribe. If you have loved ones that have crossed over and you still feel their presence, continue to cultivate that relationship. If you are drawn to certain animals, know that isn't just a preference of opinion, it's a soulful calling and connection. We have relationships with spirits, just as we do humans, but like any bond, it takes work to deepen them. Put your attention here. Learn to communicate with your guides. Fill your sacred spaces with images of the angels you love, the deities that resonate with you, the animals that your heart connects to. When shit hits the fan, it's good to have friends in high places.

A deep and sovereign relationship to our beloved Earth is a life saver too. I love to work with the four directions, along with Father Sky and Mother Earth, and the four elements of Earth, Air, Fire, and Water. I use my connection to each to create a safe and conscious container every time I do work with the medicines or when I sit down to meditate. It's the way I honor the Earth and my connection to her, by making it conscious and feeling into these vibrations. Create a ritual of connection, and when suffering comes knocking, you have the benefit of a conscious and heartfelt bond to our amazing, powerful, and protective home. This is utterly priceless—she is always there, ready and willing to help alchemize our pain, but we have to let her in.

For many of us, music is another tool that can immediately transform our energies. I have playlists that uplift me, some that create the feeling of holiness, some that make me want to dance like a maniac, and some that express the beauty of the darkness. Take the time to craft different sonic journeys for different modes. There are a handful of songs that are so precious to me, they can lift me out of the darkest corners of my mind. Music is shamanic. Let it transform you when your heart is broken. And if you're in an Ayahuasca ceremony when the darkness swirls in, know that the icaros are literally there as life rafts. The music is the primary technology we use to communicate and connect with MamaAya. It can be the savior that someone in distress needs to return to a state of heaven, but once again, we have to do the work of allowing those vibrations enter into our hearts and minds. It's not meant to be background music. Let those vibrations fill you up and rescue you from the abyss.

In the end, it's relationships that always save us. Love is what matters. So, the more we cultivate bonds with ourselves, with our spirit tribe, with our human tribe, and with our tools and techniques, the more we know unequivocally that we are not alone when hell comes to visit. We are capable of handling and transforming any experience. And we are wise to make sure we have lots of allies before the next trip to the underworld manifests.

And for all of you, I hope it does, in the safest and most life-changing way possible. This is how we expand and learn. And there is nothing I pray for all of humanity to experience more than a Spiritual Awakening.

The Earth needs us. We need us. The entire multiverse needs us. And Plant Medicines are one of the most powerful paths to connecting with our authentic badass-ery. So, if you are called, go there. Be discerning and wise and protective of your beautiful and sensitive selves, but do not let fear keep you from your destiny.

Stay safe, and journey well.

About Tina Kat Courtney

TINA "KAT" COURTNEY, also known as The AfterLife Coach, is a traditionally trained Ayahuasquera and Huachumera, carrying the Shipibo-Conibo, Quechua-Lamista, and Chavin plant medicine lineages.

She works as a ceremony guide and psychedelic integration coach and is a certified Death Doula. Kat is an enthusiastic advocate for reverent and safe plant medicine experiences and is a passionate messenger of how to co-create magic without trauma in psychedelic spaces.

She is also the co-founder of Plant Medicine People, a Plant Medicine concierge company. If you'd like to work with Kat, or join her in a Sacred Ceremony, find out more at www.afterlife.coach and www.plantmedicinepeople.com.

About the Plant Medicine Mystery School Series

THE PLANT MEDICINE MYSTERY SCHOOL is a multi-volume book series exploring the wildly mysterious and monumental power of plant consciousness. Each volume will explore a different facet of the partnership between humans and plants, honoring indigenous wisdoms as well as new scientific discoveries. This is a book series for those fascinated by the role plants play as healers, consciousness expanders, and divine beings that help to remind all those who connect with them the truth of our power to heal, expand, and love. Future volumes will include comprehensive information about topics such as the ancient tradition of Master Plant Diets, the crucial process of ceremony integration, and an intimate account of life as a shaman. The goal of each book is to further human understanding of the potentiality that lies in reverent, humble mergences with nature and all her many personalities.

About Metanoia Press

METANOIA PRESS IS AN INDEPENDENT, utopian, double-blind peer-reviewed publisher navigating the intersections between inner and outer change. Gambling that consciousness is the crux of the 21st century biscuit, the key to change on both ecological and social scales, Metanoia digs deeeeep into global and local traditions of nonduality including psychonautics, fiction, meditation, poetry, music and visual art as we collectively wake up from the evolutionary dead end of subject/object thinking and the practices of ego. With a growing global sangha of writers, editors, artists and musicians, Metanoia Press hereby composes the soundtrack to the post pandemic awakening: Tune in, Turn on, Transform.

MetanoiaPress

www.metanoia.press

www.ingramcontent.com/pod-product-compliance
Lightning Source LLC
Chambersburg PA
CBHW060018100426
42740CB00010B/1515